UNLOCKED

Unlocking Life's Myths and
Choosing to Be Free!

Leonard LaPlaca

Copyright © 2020 by Leonard LaPlaca

All rights reserved under International and Pan-American Copyright Conventions. No part of this book may be reproduced in any form or by any electronic or mechanical means including information storage and retrieval systems, without permission in writing from the publisher, except by a reviewer who may quote brief passages in a review.

ISBN: 978-1-1935142-38-6

Dedication

This book is dedicated to JoAnn, since she is not only my beloved wife, but also the best friend I have in the entire world. Also, this book is dedicated to Easton and Roman, my grandchildren, with my wishes for them being lives full of kindness, love, laughter and that their bookshelves will be full of inspirational books.

Acknowledgments

Again, I would like to thank JoAnn, my wife, who has been a positive stabilizing influence on me, and I am grateful for the tremendous sacrifices that our parents have made on our behalf. (As Robin Sharma stated, "Adore your parents. You'll miss them when they're gone.")

Also, I would like to thank Jackie, our daughter, for sharing enthusiastically her creativity with me, which enabled me to bring this book to fruition and for being the great mother that she is to our grandchildren.

In addition, our grandchildren, Easton and Roman, daily enhance our lives with their enthusiastic outlook. (Enthusiasm rightfully is the little - recognized secret of success.)

Next, Russert, our loyal and beloved dog, truly is one of our master teachers in disguise, teaching us the power of unconditional love.

Finally, thank you to my friends (especially Dwight, Joe, Jim-deceased but still in my thoughts and guiding me - Jeff, Nick, and Eric) for being an effective support system and teaching me that real life is all about relationships. As we mature (definitely not getting older), one of the really important questions we should be asking ourselves is: "Are we collecting treasures - our relationships with people - or trinkets, material possessions?"

Special thanks to Tim Schulte and *Variance Author Services* (a true professional yet amicable - a rarity in today's world) for constantly going the extra mile, to assist in the production of this book. In memory of Charles Jones because he is in a class by himself, I salute him. Even though he has been my teacher, role model, and mentor, it would be impossible to count all the ways that he assisted me. I only hope that I can return the favor to someone in the future. He has all the positive traits previously mentioned - and then some - all rolled into one person. I will always be grateful to him for his support and guidance.

Being a reverse paranoid, I am very grateful that the universe is operating on my behalf.

UNLOCKED

Unlocking Life's Myths and Choosing to Be Free!

Leonard LaPlaca

CONTENTS

Preface………………………………1

The Power………………………...5

My Goals and Promises………….12

Myth #1: The event is the determining factor in the outcome.

Reality: How you choose to respond to the event will determine the unique outcome for you. …….**30**

Myth #2: Live in the present.

Reality: Know the specific words you want on your tombstone. ……………………………………...**65**

Myth #3: Being grateful is not only the key to our success but also to our inner peace.

Reality: We need to expand our concepts about gratitude. ………………………………………**83**

Myth #4: If you can't do it well, don't do it at all.
Reality: Do it over poorly enough times until you can do it well. …………………………… **98**

Myth #5: We need to take control of our lives.
Reality: Control is a myth. …………………**112**

Myth #6: The truth will set you free.
Reality: Your truth about yourself is often false. **140**

Myth #7: We learn from our mistakes.
Reality: We learn from our mistakes only when we use the six-step process. …………………**157**

Myth #8: Show me a person who works, and I will show you a success.
Reality: Show me a person who gets excited about his/her work, and I will show you a success. ..**173**

Myth #9: Time heals all wounds.
Reality: Time, in and of itself, does not heal all wounds. …………………………………**194**

Myth #10: There are two types of thinking.
Reality: There are three types of thinking. …**219**

BONUS

SEVEN STRATEGIES TO OVERCOME FEAR AND PROTECT YOUR FUTURE BY JOANNA BRANDI 233

Endnotes..245
Suggested Reading List........................251
About the Author................................253

PREFACE

The enclosed fables, parables, quotations, and motivational human-interest stories are the nuggets of gold from the wealth of information that I have amassed since 1963. This truly has been a labor of love, and hopefully, I can continue until my dying day. Why? "School is never out for the pro!"
What should you know about me?

1. I don't have it all together.
2. I shall never have it all together.
3. I am struggling like everyone else.
4. I have made mistakes.
5. I will continue to make mistakes.
6. Presently, I am making mistakes.
7. None of these ideas are mine.
8. None of these ideas are unique.
9. If you feel anything foolish or ludicrous is said, it is I.

10. If you think anything prudent is mentioned, it is simply God channeling His wisdom through me.
11. Also, when it comes to my faith, I am strictly in the kindergarten stage.
12. Finally, if I have any gift at all, it is to break concepts down into manageable bite-size chunks so you can taste success – whatever that means to you since success is as personal as your own toothbrush. You can begin to taste success *immediately,* implementing the ideas that resonate with you.

"And once the storm is over, you won't remember how you made it through, how you managed to survive. You won't even be sure, whether the storm is really over. But one thing is certain. When you come out of the storm, you won't be the same person who walked in. That's what this storm is all about."

- *Haruki Murakami*

The Power

When I was in my sixties, I successfully completed writing my first book, even though I could not type, knew nothing about how to use a computer, and knew very little (actually zilch) about the internet. What enabled me not only to write my first book but also a second one and, most recently, my third one? The answer is the power of enthusiasm.

To illustrate, Sir Edward Appleton, whose scientific experiments and discoveries made possible worldwide broadcasting, had been knighted by the King of England, and was also awarded the Nobel Prize in Physics. In an interview, he was asked if he had any formula for success. His immediate answer was: "It was enthusiasm." Then he added, "I rate that even ahead of professional skill."

Why is enthusiam so powerful? This word comes from two Greek words: "en," meaning "within," and "theos," meaning "God." Therefore, the word literally means "God within." Can this be an unbeatable combination: God and you?

Because of the power of enthusiasm, you can be both patient and persistent at the same time. Some people incorrectly assume that if a person is patient, that person cannot be persistent, or if another person is persistent, that same person cannot be patient. However, there is such a trait as patient persistence, which enables you to be enthusiastic yet still remain patient throughout the entire process.

After reading the following story numerous times, a quotation by Orison Swett Marden came to my mind:

"This force, which is the best thing in you, your highest self, will never respond to any ordinary half-hearted call, or any milk-and-water endeavor. It can only be reached by your supremest call, your supremest effort. It will respond only to a call that is backed up by the whole of you, not part of you; you must be all there in what you are trying to do. You must bring every particle of your energy, unanswerable resolution, your best efforts, your persistent industry to your task or the best will not come out of you. You must back up your ambition by your whole nature, by unbounded enthusiasm and determination to win which knows no failure… Only a masterly call, a masterly will, a supreme effort, intense and persistent application, can unlock the door to your inner treasure and release your highest powers."

This story exemplifies "THIS FORCE" in action and is one of the most inspirational non-religious stories that I have ever encountered. The Brooklyn Bridge that spans the river between

Manhattan and Brooklyn is simply an engineering miracle. In 1883 a creative engineer, John Roebling, was inspired by an idea for the spectacular bridge project. However, bridge-building experts told him to forget it, since it just was not possible. An old joke defines an expert.

"One type of expert has been defined as: Ex = has been, Spurt = small drip under pressure."

Roebling convinced his son, Washington, an up-and-coming engineer, that the bridge could be built. Belief is power! The two of them conceived the concept of how it could be accomplished, and how to overcome the obstacles. Because of their unbridled enthusiasm, they convinced bankers to finance the project. Now, with unharnessed excitement and energy, they hired their crew and began to build their dream bridge.

The project was only a few months underway when a dreadful on-site accident killed John Roebling and severely injured his son. Washington was severely brain-damaged, unable to talk or walk. Everyone thought that the project would have to be scrapped, since the Roeblings were the only ones who understood how the bridge could be built. What would have you done in this situation?

Though Washington Roebling was unable to move or talk, his mind was as sharp as ever. He still had a fierce determination

(DDR = DETERMINATION DETERMINES RESULTS!)

to complete the bridge. One day, as he lay in his hospital bed, an idea flashed in his mind as to how to develop a communication code. All he could move was one finger, so he touched the arm of his wife with that finger. He meticulously tapped out the code to communicate to her what she was to tell the engineers who continued building the bridge. For 13 years (Is that hard to believe?) Washington enthusiastically (Work is not work if you enjoy it!) tapped out his instructions with one finger until the spectacular Brooklyn Bridge was finally completed.[1] Could the only handicap you ever have be in your own mind?

Finally, for over 20 years, part of my personal philosophy has been Kaizen, a Japanese word meaning continuous improvement or change for the better, which is made of two characters in Japanese: kai, which means "change," and zen, which means "good." Kaizen is a twofold process, since it entails your being a little better each day and doing a little more each day through not only taking positive actions but also the help and support of other people, who understand - as exemplified in the following quotation by Patricia Sun - that we are all in this together.

"When you understand that the world is round, you can never choose up sides!" - Patricia Sun

FOOD FOR THOUGHT

*"If an egg is broken by an outside force, life ends. If broken by an inside force, life begins. Great things always begin from the inside."
Jim Kwik*

Since improvement has no limits, I never want to stop trying to improve. Hopefully, my next book will be better than this one, since the best is yet to be!

My Goals and Promises

Thank you for taking the time - <u>one of your most valuable possessions</u> - not only to purchase this book, but also to scrutinize meticulously this pertinent information. Please "run" with the ideas that click with you, not only using them now, but even showing and teaching them to the members of your family and support groups. This is how you earn the highest rate of retention, by using and sharing/teaching the concepts to others. However, if any idea does not appear to be beneficial, do not discard it, but instead store it in your brain for future use. Who knows - days, weeks, months, or years from now-that same idea might prove to be very advantageous to you? If you immediately dispose of any idea, no imprint is left on your brain. Then, if you attempted to retrieve that information at any future date, it would be an impossibility because of the lack of an imprint, since that idea was thrown away instantly. Finally, I have four promises that I am making to each of you with the contents of this book.

My goals:
1. To both motivate and inspire you
2. To inspire you to take positive action Now!
3. To give you "positive goosebumps"
4. To share startling, good news about life

In my first book ***Fountains of Life. Choose the Life You Want to Live***, Noah Martin, a writer and true friend, and I shared the following insightful truths about motivation:

1. Motivation is a personal commitment to yourself to be the best person you can be. Can anyone ask for anything more?

2. Motivation is an inner energy that moves you to accomplish tasks and goals.

3. Motivation is an attitude about life that gives you the belief you can make a difference in this world.

4. Motivation is a powerful belief that your life is significant, and that you can do effective things with it for the good of others and for the benefit of the world. Belief is power!

5. Motivation is an agreement with your Creator to work with him to nudge the world toward greater goodness and purpose. Can this be an unbeatable combination - God and you?

First, motivation will provide you with the needed endurance, as you deal effectively with your difficulties and adversities. Motivation not only gives hope but also leads to the proper actions, converting your hope into reality. Even though motivation is important, since it unquestionably helps you to achieve your goals, I am here not only to motivate you, but also to inspire you. The word inspiration comes from the Latin word "inspirare" which means "spirit" or "divine guidance." Inspiration can be compared to a fire, a fire that is lit in your heart. As long as your heart chakra (heart energy center) remains open, that fire will never go out, because you will be "filled with spirit." Please remember that neither motivation nor inspiration is a bad thing, and we can utilize them to help us to continue to move onward, upward, and forward. The following quotation by Wayne Dyer clarifies how motivation and inspiration both complement and supplement each other:

*"**Motivation is when you get hold of an idea and carry it through to its conclusion, and inspiration is when an idea gets hold of you and carries you where you are intended to go.**"*

Secondly, I am here to promote you to act, because ideas are worthless, unless we act upon them.

IQ is more important than IQ
IQ > IQ

In the preceding statement, notice we have a greater than sign to remind us that the second IQ (INTELLIGENCE QUOTIENT) is not as important as the first IQ (IMPLEMENTATION QUOTIENT). This is not good news but startling, good news. Why? We do not have total control over our intelligence quotient because of the genetic factor and certain environmental influences, but we do have control over our implementation quotient.

We hear it said, "knowledge is power", which is a fallacy because knowledge, only if properly applied, is power. However, knowledge without implementation is useless; knowledge with implementation is priceless.

Also, I am hoping to inspire you to take positive action right NOW, since NOW is WON spelled backwards. The following (which can be found in my first book mentioned above), exemplifies how we can help people by taking immediate positive action rather than procrastinate.

In "***The Hole***", a parable, a man is walking through a dark area, and inadvertently falls into a mammoth hole. He struggles and struggles to get out, but all his attempts are in vain.

Finally, he realized he needed help. Does this sound like all of us? In despair, he sat down, despondent, and buried his head in his hands. Shortly, he heard footsteps above, and he bellowed for help. After stopping and walking to the edge, the people there instantly began to lecture him about the dangers, especially alone, of walking through sinister areas. Then, they walked on. Next, a doctor stopped, gave him a prescription for pain, and told him to call his office - when he got out - for an appointment. Then, a lawyer walking by noticed the man, gave him his card, and told him to call his office so they could sue the city on his behalf. Later, a priest noticed the same man and told him he would say a special prayer for him as soon as he arrived at the church. When a common man (NO SUCH THING) noticed the man, he jumped in with him. Notice he did not check out the age, race, religion, nationality, sex, background, or affluence of the person, but simply saw a person in dire need of help. The man, originally in the hole, said, "What are you doing? Now there are two of us stuck in the hole."

"No," the other man replied. "I have been here before, and I know the way out." So, both men climbed out of the hole together. Notice the man who jumped in didn't lecture or offer any type of advice, but he did something more drastic and effective.

This story shows the power of so-called ordinary people helping each other and is not a put-down of doctors, lawyers and the clergy.

In a similar parable entitled *"The Pit"*, 20 different people saw the man in the pit but took no positive action on his behalf. Finally, Jesus, seeing the man, took him by the hand and lifted him out of the pit. Should we not daily follow the same course of action?

Thirdly, I am excited to share with you fables, parables, quotations, motivational and inspirational human-interest stories that, hopefully, will not only give you "positive goose bumps" but also will encourage you to take positive actions right now and – if you are receptive – be your own rallying cry.

Even though I came across the following in the 2019 editions of The Winners' Journal as well as the Christian Winners' Journal by Dr. John and Pam Carls, they still enhance today positive vibrations in me which, hopefully, will enable me to be involved in the highest form of living that there is - GIVING WITH NO STRINGS ATTACHED. I hope that you relish **"The Joy Bag," "The Carpenter,"** and

"The Box" as well as the quotation by Einstein, as much as I do.

The Joy Bag

I went to a luncheon and was given a **Joy Bag**. I would like to share this **Joy Bag** with you, wishing you a bag full of happiness!

In this **Joy Bag** is:

A **Penny** so you will never have to say, "I'm broke"
A **Rubber Band** to stretch yourself beyond your limits
A **Cotton Ball** for the rough roads to remind you to seek the cushioned support of family and friends
A **Tootsie Roll** to remind you to roll with the punches
A **Marble** for when you lose yours
A **Starburst** to give you a burst of energy on days when you don't have any
A **Chocolate Kiss** to remind you that you are loved
A **Crayon** to color your day bright
A **Bandaid** for when things get a little rough
An **Eraser** to remind you that you can start every day with a clean slate

A **Paper Clip** to help keep things together when they are out of control

A small **Smooth Stone** to remind you that the rough times help to refine and polish

A **Star** to remind you to shine and that you are the best

A **Stick of Gum** to remind you to stick to it

A **String** to tie things together when everything falls apart

A **PUZZLE PIECE** - WITHOUT YOU, THINGS WOULDN'T BE COMPLETE [1]

The Carpenter

An elderly carpenter was ready to retire. He told his employer-contractor of his plans to leave the house building business and live a more leisurely life with his wife enjoying his extended family. He would miss the paycheck, but he needed to retire. They could get by.

The contractor was sorry to see his good worker go and asked if he could build just one more house as a personal favor. The carpenter said yes, but in time it was easy to see that his heart was not in his work. He resorted to shoddy workmanship and used inferior materials. It was an unfortunate way to end his career.

When the carpenter finished his work and the builder came to inspect the house, the contractor handed the front-door key to the carpenter. "This is your house," he said, "my gift to you."

What a shock! What a shame! If he had only known he was building his own house, he would have done it all so differently. Now he had to live in the home that he had built none too well.

So, it is with us.

We build our lives in a distracted way, reacting rather than acting, willing to put forth with less than the best. At important points we do not give the job our best effort. Then with a shock we look at the situation we have created and find that we are now living in the house we have built. If we had realized that we would have done it differently.

Think of yourself as the carpenter. Think about your house. Each day you hammer a nail, place a board, or erect a wall. Build it wisely.

It is the only life you will ever build. Even if you only live it for only one day more, that day deserves to be lived graciously and with dignity.

The plaque on the wall says, "Life is a do-it-yourself project."

Who could say it more clearly? Your life today is the result of your attitudes and choices in the past. Your life tomorrow will be the result of your attitudes and the choices you make today.[2]

-Author Unknown

The Box

One day I was sitting around the pool talking with a couple of friends. One friend said, "Each of us is given a box. It is set in front of us. It contains challenges, opportunities, and setbacks."

We never know what, when, where, or why these will occur. It is up to us to deal with the circumstances and conditions that we've been given. We use our setbacks and challenges to make us stronger. It sometimes makes us grow and takes us out of our comfort zone in the process. It definitely makes us examine our values and priorities. It may take a while for us to rebound and land on your feet, but when we do, we will learn from our experience and the process. It is up to us to use our

God-given talents and personalities to deal with the situation at hand.

We may attack the situation head on or we may procrastinate awhile before we deal with it. How we respond to the challenges, opportunities, and setbacks determine who we are and who we become.

-Pam Carls

What kind of box do you see?
A Moving Box? A Tool Box?
A Treasure Box? A Gift Box?
What you see defines who you are and who you become.[3]

"Life is like riding a bicycle. To keep your balance you must keep moving."[4]
Albert Einstein

My final promise to you is that I shall be sharing startling, good news based on the following four great premises, which I have been discovering because of my readings and the course of giving speeches since 1963.

1. Right now, each of you is wiser, braver, and more intelligent than you think you are.

2. Right now, each of you - one person - can make a positive difference in today's world.

3. Little things make the big difference in the world.

4. Real life is not doing what you like to do but what you need to do and ought to do.

The format for the book will be as follows:

1. Poignant Quote
2. The Myth
3. The Reality
4. Food for Thought

"No psychological fear is part of your original equipment."
Guy Finley

MYTH #1:

THE EVENT IS THE DETERMINING FACTOR IN EACH OUTCOME IN YOUR LIFE.

REALITY:

HOW YOU CHOOSE TO RESPOND TO EACH EVENT WILL DETERMINE THE UNIQUE OUTCOME IN YOUR LIFE.

I would like to share with you my four deep, dark secrets that have emphasized how I choose to respond to each event determined a unique outcome for me.

1. 1960s - nervous breakdown with numerous shock treatments
2. July 2, 2001 - the death of our 20 - year - old son (dead in his bed in our home)
3. 2011 - generalized anxiety and panic attacks
4. 2014 - generalized anxiety, panic attacks and agoraphobia (abnormal fear of being in public places and leaving your home)

Throughout the years, I have been learning that keeping secrets often prevents me from coping with problems at hand and does lead to the **"THREE - HEADED MONSTER" (FEAR - WORRY - ANXIETY)** which can dominate my life. Since I am focusing on these events, I am making them appear to be more important than they really are. However, if I "expose them to the light" by sharing them with people that I respect and turn them over to God (still willing to do my part), the power of these secrets begins to dissipate. Revealing secrets (sharing/writing) enables me to think about them more effectively and makes me feel better.

    Pertaining to the first event (nervous breakdown with numerous shock treatments in the 1960s), I assumed that I earned this breakdown because of my being a worryaholic, workaholic, and a perfectionist! I did not realize at the time that what happened to me could have been a combination of biological imbalance and psychological distortion, which could have been triggered by any number of factors. After receiving numerous shock treatments, lying in bed and with time to ponder my situation, it slowly dawned on me that if my misdirected negative thinking got me here, then I could turn my life around by focusing on the positives and practicing the power of positive expectations which would lead to my center. How was I to accomplish this? "When the student is ready, the teacher will appear." Eventually, I came across this quote in **"Life is Tremendous!"** by Charles Jones:

"You will be the same in five years as you are today except for the people you meet and the books you read."[1]

Other statements in the book jumped out at me such as:

"The mark of a person who is growing is his understanding that things go wrong to make us more right. God never breaks a man down with problems except to build him up."[2]

As well as,

"I've been learning that while I can't determine in life when i'm going to get kicked,

I can determine which way i'm going to go when I get kicked." [3]

Those inspirational words hit a raw nerve in me. Remembering a quotation, I came across by Norman Vincent Peale about shampooing your brain every morning, I realized my mission was twofold:

- ***ELIMINATING NEGATIVE WEEDS IN MY MIND*** - not my drinking that got me stinking but my "stinking thinking" that got me drinking
- ***PLANTING POSITIVE SEEDS***

Nature abhors a vacuum. If we simply eliminate negative thoughts, other mental weeds will take control, unless we plant positive seeds. I planted the seeds by reading motivational, inspirational, religious, spiritual, psychological, and self - help books. Since I have a very nasty habit of attempting to accomplish too much too quickly, I divided my major goal into mini - goals, small manageable bite - size chunks. By reading an X number of books per year during that 20-year period, I was "slicing" ("the salami approach to solving problems - one slice at a time") my goal and immediately "tasting success." I met my goal and have been "hooked" on reading ever since. I have also used the writers and people mentioned in the books not only as my mentors but also as my "psychological parents" and thus developed my own unique support system. We cannot do it alone. According to the Italian artist Luciano de Crescenzo *"We are each of us angels with only one wing and we can only fly embracing each other."* We need the help and support of other people. Even the Lone Ranger had Tonto, his friend, and Silver, his horse. There are numerous benefits of effective support groups such as gaining a better understanding of yourself, learning pertinent information, as well as realizing that other people have similar concerns. This can be very enjoyable and rewarding.

Pertaining to my nervous breakdown, how did God enter the scene on my behalf, remembering that His ways are not our ways?

"For my thoughts are not your thoughts,
Neither are your ways my ways,"
says the Lord.
"For as the heavens are higher than the earth so are my ways higher than your ways and my thoughts are not your thoughts." **Isaiah 55:8-9**

Right after my second year of teaching, I had earned a scholarship for a two-week period at a university in Pennsylvania. 30 books were placed in front of each of the participants that we had to read during that two-week time-period. After an exhausting but stimulating year of teaching, I must have been overwhelmed, when I saw the magnitude of books. You can "milk" teaching and make it one of the easiest professions in the world, or you can make it one of the most demanding - all tied in with your inner standards. I was informed that one of my very good friends, Joe Oresko, did drive me to the hospital in Johnstown, PA, where I received numerous shock treatments. God has been very patient yet persistent with me throughout the years. God's timing was perfect since this incident happened immediately after the school year was over. Therefore, I had time to recover externally and was able to return to teaching the following year.

    At the time I was teaching in a small town in Pennsylvania. Could you fathom what might have happened if this would have occurred during the school year? Possibly, my teaching career would have been over after only a few years of teaching. TEACHING IS ONE OF MY PASSIONS! Another way that God entered the scene was that the shock treatments almost eliminated my past recollections. Was this a blessing or a curse? Who knows what is good or bad? Allow me to share a story with you that illustrates the importance of suspending judgment.

The following is an adaption of a Chinese parable about an elderly farmer/woodcutter, his only son, and his majestic white horse, which oozed poise, confidence, and enthusiasm, especially when it did gallop. The stunning white horse had a "princely" nature about it. A king in a nearby province offered him an exorbitant amount of money for the horse, but he adamantly refused. A wealthy merchant came through the area and offered the elderly man a pension for life if he would give him the horse. Indefatigably, he refused the proposal. Finally, a nobleman, going through the territory, told the farmer that he would give his son a good-paying job for the horse. Decisively, he rejected the notion. His line of reasoning was that the horse was not a possession but, instead, a friend. "You do not sell people."

The people in his village constantly used one word to describe him: *stupid or crazy*. The people knew that the farmer/woodcutter was elderly and very poor in terms of material possessions. Also, they knew that he would be given a massive amount of money for his resplendent horse, but the elderly farmer always refused all offers.

Irrelevant of the weather or of how the farmer felt, he was in the woods daily, cutting wood and selling it as firewood in the nearby hamlets.

So far, the key words are "irrelevant of the weather or of how the farmer felt." Why? If you wait until the perfect day, weather-wise, you won't get much done. Also, most of the work in this world is done by people who don't feel well. So, if you wait until you feel perfectly fine and for the perfect day weather-wise, you won't get much accomplished.

One Monday morning, the farmer was walking toward the barn and noticed the stable door was open. His horse was gone! Immediately, his neighbors came running over to tell him how stupid he was, informing him that he could have received a massive amount of money for the horse, but now the horse had been stolen.

The farmer would tell his neighbors:

"Suspend judgment!"

He would then give them a quizzical look and say, "Who knows if this is good news or bad news? Who knows if this is a blessing or a curse? The fact is that my horse is gone. This is only one sentence in one paragraph. We have not read the entire book. We are not alone in this."

His neighbors walked away, muttering among themselves about how stupid the farmer was.

About one week later, his horse returned with 12 beautiful wild stallions. Quickly, the neighbors came running over, informing him that they heard the good news about not only his horse but also of the wild stallions returning with him.

However, again, the elderly farmer responded:

"Suspend judgment!"

Then he would give them another probing stare and say, "Who knows if this is good news or bad news? Who knows if this is a blessing or a curse? The fact is that my horse returned with other wild stallions. This is only one paragraph in one chapter. We have not read the entire book. We are not alone in this."

His neighbors walked away, saying nothing outwardly but inwardly thinking how stupid the farmer was.

Nearly ten days later, his only son, in his attempts to domesticate the wild horses, was thrown, broke both of his legs, and became permanently crippled.

Expeditiously, the neighbors informed him how sorry they felt about the plight of his family since now the farmer would have to take care of his son because of his crippled condition.

Without any hesitation, the farmer responded:

"Suspend judgment!"

At that instant, he would give them another prying stare and say, "Who knows if this is good news or bad news? Who knows if this is a blessing or a curse? The fact is my son was thrown from one of the horses and broke both of his legs. This is only one chapter in the book. We have not read the entire book. We are not alone in this."

Before we go on to the next incident, please remember what is true of those wild horses is also true of us. According to Charles Jones in **Life Is Tremendous:**

That wild stallion may look beautiful on the mesa with its mane blowing in the wind, but he isn't much use until someone breaks him so he can pull a load or carry a rider.

Neither is a person much good until he is harnessed to teamwork and disciplined to guidance. God trains a man so the man can run free. That's an old law; you can fight it, but you'll never change it. [4]

Finally, a warlord came into the area and conscripted all the healthy males to fight in a useless war, where all of them might be killed. However, the farmer's son was not taken because of his crippled condition.

Frantically, his neighbors came running over, with their tales of gloom and doom, telling him how fortunate he was since his son was left behind while their sons would be fighting in a needless war.

However, again, the farmer immediately retorted:

"Suspend judgment!"

After giving them an inquisitive look, he said, "Who knows if this is good news or bad news? Who knows if this is a blessing or a curse? The fact is that your sons are fighting in a war. This is only a portion of the book. We have not read the entire book. We are not alone in this."

What can we learn from the responses of the elderly farmer toward the adversities that his family encountered?

1. Equanimity (a calm patience toward all things) is the dominant trait that the farmer chose to incorporate into his daily living. What is so

pertinent about this? Each of us has this inner wisdom, this innate knowledge. However, your inner wisdom can only be unlocked when you are relaxed and calm.

Ponder the following quotations, which illustrate the power of equanimity:

"There is a huge amount of freedom that comes to you when you take nothing personally."

-Miguel Ruiz

"You always own the option of having no opinion. There is never any need to get worked up or trouble your soul about things you can't control. These things are not asking to be judged by you. Leave them alone." - **Marcus Aurelius**

"A modern definition of equanimity: cool. This refers to one whose mind remains stable and calm in all situations." **-Allan Lokos**

"He who has mastered the true nature of life does not labor over what life cannot do. He who has mastered the true nature of fate does not labor over what knowledge cannot change." **-Zhuangzi**

"Equanimity is the hallmark of spirituality. It is neither chasing nor avoiding but just being in the middle."-**Amit Ray**

2. The elderly farmer fathomed that life is a series of mysteries. Thus, his job was not to attempt to comprehend them (This is when we could go crazy!), but to be flexible — to

roll with them — and, above all, to keep the faith.

3. Finally, the elderly farmer practiced the power of positive expectations. He looked for the good (the lessons/gifts) in every situation. This is not positive thinking but choosing to focus on the positives in every situation while being aware of the negatives. You can daily keep your enthusiasm at a healthy high by expecting the best.

How was this a blessing, almost decimating my recollections of my past history? God knows what I can handle and what I cannot. Even if I were Superman, I could not carry the three time periods at the same time:
- Past
- Present
- Future

Therefore, almost all of my past history was annihilated, so that I could focus on the present. While I was writing my first book, I had to check with my beloved sister, Jo, and other family members and friends to obtain the relevant facts about the tenacity of my father when dealing with his horrid mining accident, the benignity of my mother, who willingly (did it out of love rather than responsibility) became his private duty nurse until his dying day and the audacity of my sister when coping successfully with her polio challenges. By almost abolishing my recall of my past history, God was working in my favor. Experts tell us that we should spend 90 percent of our time in the present and only five percent in the past and five percent in the future. Why?

"The past is history, the future is a mystery, but today is the gift. That is why it is called the present - a present from God." – Bill Keane

Why not daily use Christ's prayer as your motto? "Give us this day our daily bread." Notice the emphasis is on the present (today's bread) and not on the expired bread we ate yesterday, nor problems taking place in the future where we might not have any bread to eat at all.

Since God knows what I can handle (decidedly cannot carry the three time periods - past, present, and future - at the same time), he did almost erase my past. This was one of the gifts I received from my shock treatments. In every situation, you will find positives along with the negatives, but what do you choose to focus on? Look for the messages in the mess.

The following was created by Jeff Philibin, a former student who has become a friend — a true friend:

This day is a gift from God. it is the only way to see it. There is no other way.
This being true, then there is no "good" or "bad," as I would judge them, only ways to grow, learn, and give glory. What I would see as good or bad is only by my limited judgment. I don't know everything—God does. I don't control everything—God does. Who loves me more? I must trust him. He either makes it happen or lets it happen. So, I must trust and not question, only to open and understand the gift, which is the precious present. This day is a gift from God. It is the only way to see it. There is no other way.

I will question. I will fail to see. I will doubt, flounder, and struggle. I may even make a big enough mess of things that there may seem to be no way forward. But that is due to my limits, not God's. When this happens, I will not panic or become despondent but reset myself and carry on. I will relax and realize this too is part of life, and that failures are mileposts on the road to success. I will prayfully give thanks for this sign of progress—ask for his help to learn, to see, to understand, and to persevere. And I will press on with a cheerful heart. The present is always a gift to those who choose to open it with true eyes. It is the only way to see it. There is no other way.

Along the road, I will need help and guidance. I will need to laugh and enjoy. I will need to rest and recharge. Though I possess great power and I am indeed God's greatest miracle, I am a man. I am not a machine, and I am not invincible. Though I possess great potential, I have been given the gift of limits too. I must accept this and be good to myself and others. Everyone I meet is fighting a tough battle. I must be kind. When I feel small, I must give. When I am feeling doubt, fear, powerlessness, or anxiety, I must give. I must always give because it is in giving that we are truly living. And I need to live. I must accept too for others need to live as well. I am here for good, and whatever good I can do, I must. It is the way. There is no other way.

I must live without regret. Being one person, I can only choose one path. This is also a gift, the gift of free will and choice. I will do my best to choose wisely, and then I will put my hand and heart to the task. I do not work alone. If things turn out the way I hope, I will give thanks. If they do not, I will realize that there is a gift in this too, and I must open it with true eyes. It is not a mistake; it is life! It's okay. Success is not permanent, and failure is not fatal. I will balance myself with tough-minded optimism. I will be beset on all sides with struggles, trials, challenges, and difficulties of all kinds, as winds from all directions. Yet it is that very wind that strengthens me, so I will give thanks, especially in the storm. If I struggle or despair, I will be gentle with myself and recognize that I am human. I will plant grass—positive thoughts—and strengthen my mind. I will be fearless. Not because there is nothing to fear but because I have Him who has overcome all. *All. Not most—all.* He made a way out of no way, and with Him, I cannot fail. I will love, laugh, and live without fear or regret. There is no other way.

And when do I do this, then I'm living![5]

"*You can tell the size of your God by looking at the size of your worry list. The longer your list, the smaller your God.*"
Author Unknown

Deep Dark Secret #2

On July 4, 2001, JoAnn (my wife) and I found Matt, our 20 - year - old son, dead in his bed in our home. Several years before my son's death I visited a funeral home, because the son of one of my friends had died at an early age. I informed the father that ultimately "TIME HEALS ALL WOUNDS," and eventually he would get over his son's death. Then, and justly so, the forlorn father verbally blasted me and vehemently informed me that I had no idea what he was going through, and that he would never totally get over his son's death. You will never discern how low I felt when I left the funeral home. Today, I still have a "sour taste" in my mouth/mind when I envision this incident.

    The death of my son exemplifies how naive I was at the age of 60. I truly believed that if I were a good Christian (not saying that I was), nothing diabolical would happen to my family. Could you decipher how shocked I was when JoAnn, my wife, and I found our son? Going back to how unenlightened I was at the age of 60 referring to grief and the grief recovery process, I decided to embark on a new journey by utilizing one of my very few strong points which is my love/passion for reading. Since 2001 (after the death of my son), I have consumed many (stopped counting at 50) books on grief and the grief recovery process. I plan to continue reading on this issue until my dying day.

Presently, I have numerous books on grief and have given away myriad books on this topic.

Also, when there is a death in the family of anyone that I know (have been doing this since 2001) I do send them a "CARE PACKAGE," consisting of a detailed explanation of the grief recovery process and brochures on any of the following topics, dependent on the needs of the people.

Some of the titles are as follows:
Grieving as a Woman – Kass P. Dotterweich
Handling Grief as a Man - Bob Miller
Getting Through the first weeks after a Funeral – Herbert Weber
Making Sense Out of Suffering – Jack Wentz O.F.M.
Grieving the Loss of a Grown Son or Daughter – Carol Luebering
When a Death Comes Unexpectedly – Larry A. Platt

What to Say to Someone who Has Cancer – Patti Normile

Bearing the Special Grief of Suicide – Arnaldo Pangrazzi

Finding God in Pain or Illness – Susan Saint Sing

Helping a Child to Grieve and Grow – Carol Luebering

The Ten Biggest Myths about Grief – Kay Talbot PhD

Also, the brilliant books by Earl Hipp on this topic include:

Fighting Invisible Tigers (Stress Management for Teens)

Feed Your Head (Some Excellent Stuff On Being Yourself)-The Caring Circle

and my all-time favorite

Help for The Hard Times (Getting through Loss) which contains the following:

Seven Things a Grieving Person Needs to Know

1.   You are loveable even when you are a confused mess.

2.   Crying is a gift.

3.   Almost every thought, feeling, and behavior is normal.

4.   You are not alone.

5.   People are uncomfortable with grieving people.

6.   No matter how bad you feel you will survive.

7.   It takes as long as it takes. [6]

I have dubbed this (sending out packets of information) "Matt's (my son's first name) Ministry," and I thank Matt each time that I do this. In this way on Matt's behalf, I am hoping to leave a minute positive thumbprint here on this earth. If Matt would not have died when I was 60, I still today, at 79, would be that same naive person appertaining to grief and the grief recovery process.

In every situation you will find positives along with negatives but what do you choose to focus on?

Since I am doing this ("Matt's Ministry") with all of my effort, energy, passion, with all my heart and with complete love, I have been becoming - in this respect - a *"MERAKLIS!"* Meraki is a modern Greek word but is derived from the Turkish "Merak" which entails doing something with passion, love, soul, and creativity.

Finally, deep dark secrets three and four

Because of my panic attacks and generalized anxiety in 2011 and 2014 along with agoraphobia in 2014, I declared an "ALL OUT WAR" against negativity. This is a war that cannot be won. Again, for the third time in my life, I turned to one of my few strong points - my passion for reading.

Reading properly will provide you with many more benefits, including relaxation, rather than passively watching television. Reading gives you control since you get to choose the time, place, pace, and selection of material, which is almost limitless. Depending on what you read, you can benefit from the experiences of other people — both their successes and failures. Finally, since reading properly is an active thought-provoking process, you are exercising your brain muscle as you read. (**A few of the books that I have been reading are listed at the back of the book.**)

Why, after all these years, haven't I been winning this war against negativity? One primary reason is because I have been focusing on the negatives in my life and, therefore, earning additional negatives. Why? "What you think about, expands." Since I have been focusing on negatives, I have been garnering additional negatives. Also, as Carl Jung says, *"Whatever you resist persists."*

Since I have been resisting negativity, it has been persisting. Finally, and it has been taking me my entire life to infer this, the way that God devised the universe is magnificent. Why? For every negative emotion, He set up a corresponding positive emotion that we can substitute for the negative one. Instead of SORROW, we can interchange **JOY**. Why not replace **CHEER** for GLOOM or **GRATITUDE** for COMPLAINT? Also, we can replace **FORGIVENESS** for GUILT, **DETERMINATION** for RESIGNATION, and **FAITH** for WORRY. Now, when confronted with negative thoughts, I accept them, acknowledge them, but then immediately say "CANCEL - CANCEL" and select a positive emotion to eradicate the negative. I definitely am not saying that the ***"BLACK DOG"*** (used as a metaphor for melancholy or depression) will never envelop my life again, but, hopefully, with these God - given strategies, (especially the one previously mentioned - the power of substitution) I shall be able to reduce the destructive effects of fear, worry, and anxiety in my life and bounce back from these "bumps in the road" much quicker and continue to move onward, upward, and forward, since life is movement.

FOOD FOR THOUGHT

Even though we are taught to convert our lemons into lemonade, instead embrace our lemons, hug them, and immediately look for the lessons/gifts, and messages rather than declaring an all - out war on them, performing radical surgery on them, and slicing/dicing them into lemonades.

Len LaPlaca

HELP FOR THE HARD TIMES:

- Don't "do" anything. ("Don't run from the heart. Don't get away from it all.")
- Remember, grief is normal and healthy.
- Don't try to keep it all together.

- If you need help, get it.
- Be yourself no matter what.
- Cry if you can.
- Take care of your body.
- Keep it simple.
- Let time pass.
- Be with caring people.
- Talk, Talk, Talk.
- Get a guide.
- Ask for support.
- Take some time alone.
- Lean on your spirituality. [7]

"And we know that in all things God works for the good of those who love him, who have been called according to his purpose."
Romans 8:28

Could Romans 8:28 be the most encouraging verse in the Bible, because it helps us to comprehend the momentous and decisive importance of loving God through everything - THE GOOD, THE BAD, AND THE UGLY?

"If our testimonies are strong on this point, and if we feel the absolute assurance that God loves us, we will change our questions. We won't ask, 'Why did this happen?' or 'Why doesn't God care about me?' Instead, our questions will become, 'What can I learn from this experience?' or 'How does the Lord want me to handle this?'"
John Bytheway

MYTH #2:
LIVE IN THE PRESENT.

REALITY:
LIVING IN THE PRESENT IS PERTINENT, BUT YOU SHOULD ALSO KNOW THE SPECIFIC WORDS YOU WANT ON YOUR TOMBSTONE.

The following parable exemplifies how we can choose to focus on the good, the positive, and the present, irrelevant of any situation that we encounter.

One day, a monk was in the jungle, gathering fruit. When he came upon a tiger, the petrified monk dropped his basket and ran away as quickly as possible. Unfortunately, the tiger began to pursue him to the top of the cliff. As the monk pensively looked back, he noticed that the tiger was gaining ground on him and would soon pounce on him. Fortunately, the monk then noticed a vine hanging from the top of a cliff. Hastily he grabbed hold of it and swung over the edge, bracing himself against its rocky side. Carefully he began to descend, only to see another tiger waiting for him at the bottom of the cliff. Then, to add to his dilemma, two mice, a black one and a white one, came from a crevice in the side of the cliff and began to nibble at the vine. As he was about to be overcome by fear, the monk noticed right beside him a strawberry plant growing from a crack in the cliff. He grabbed it with his one hand and ate the most luscious strawberry he had ever tasted. For that one moment, the monk's fear was temporarily diverted as he savored the most delicious fruit he had ever eaten.

You can only have one dominant thought at a time--focus, focus, focus! After the monk did everything physically and intellectually possible to escape the tigers, he made a choice to live in the present.

The monk found a ledge to lean on, and eventually the tigers became tired of waiting and left for a timelier meal. The man, now very humbled, made his way up the cliff and escaped safely through the jungle back to his hamlet.

For many days, the monk reflected on his horrifying experience. Tribulations never leave you where they found you. You will change, becoming better or bitter. He determined that he would make a choice to live in the present and to focus on the good things around him that he could enjoy in the moment. From that day onward, the man was constantly looking for windows of opportunity.

"Opportunity knocks" is a false idea. You are opportunity. You must take the initiative. You must go to the door and open the door. If you are not worth a rap, will opportunity knock?

The monk was elated and grateful that he was alive. He had learned many important lessons from his near-death or, you might say, his life-opening experience. He realized how truly fragile life is and vowed that he would never put off living again. The monk sensed that he discovered the strawberries (gifts) in his life because of the tigers. The tigers forced him off his beaten path, where eventually he discovered hidden gifts (strawberries). He also became aware of the tigers in his life but made a conscious choice not to focus on them. Instead, he focused on the strawberries, thereby earning additional strawberries. "What you think about expands."

From the traumatic happenings (tigers) to the little, nagging, and everyday problems (mice), we can learn to focus on the good and the true and thus bring meaning and hope to our lives. Some people, including myself, tend to focus on the bad things that have happened or the bad things that they think will happen and fail to see the beauty of life right in front of them. If you reach out and grasp the beauty in a bleak situation, you might discover happiness. From his experience, the monk developed an inner wisdom that enabled him to live life with calmness, awareness, and thoughtfulness. He developed more of a passion for life that would only increase in meaning and purpose.

Some experts tell us that we have not begun to live until we can precisely tell other people what we want on our tombstone - in three words or less. My three words would be: **HAPPY-HUNGRY-HUMBLE.** Pertaining to happiness I have chosen to be happy - right now. According to Norman Vincent Peale, *"Our most important power is the power of choice."* Happiness, as well as love, is not a feeling but a choice, several choices. When most people think of happiness they think of the ABCs (ADDING-BUILDING-CONSTRUCTING), but in reality, happiness is a ridding/shedding process. We want to eliminate the ANTs (AUTOMATIC NEGATIVE THOUGHTS) in our minds not by resisting them, ("What you resist persists."), but by substituting positive loving thoughts in their place. One of the keys to happiness is not as much being loved, as it is to send out positive loving thoughts to others. Why? We emphatically do not have total control over being loved, but we do have total control over sending out positive loving thoughts to others. Since we are focusing on positive loving thoughts, we will earn additional positives in our lives.

"What we appreciate, appreciates."- Lynne Twist

We will then discern that one person - by sending out these positive loving thoughts - can make positive contributions in our world. This will boost our confidence and enhance our efforts. I am totally content and happy with my material possessions and I firmly believe that things, especially material things, do not make people happy, as illustrated in the following story.

Imagine a young lady whose family's lifestyle could be summarized in one word - CORPULENT. On her 21st birthday, she was given a birthday cake by her parents. Meticulously wrapped around each of the 21 candles was a one-thousand-dollar bill - a total of $21,000 for her birthday. However, two weeks later she committed suicide leaving this note to her parents:

Mom and Dad,

All my life

you have given

me everything

to live my

life with (referring

to material items)

but nothing to

live my life for.

She printed her last sentence three times the size of her previous sentence to get her final message across to her parents:

I WAS ALWAYS

ALONE IN THIS BIG

HOUSE!!

Love, to our loved ones, is spelled time, not money, not material items and or possessions, but **TIME**. Is there such a thing as unconditional happiness? Suspend judgment and read Michael A. Singer's stimulating book *The Untethered Soul* before you answer.

Even though I am happy, I am hungry and, hopefully, will continue to be hungry until my dying day for these five things:

1. Learning
2. Growing
3. Sharing
4. Reaching out to other people
5. Drawing nearer to God

The following straight line illustrates one of the biggest fallacies about life.

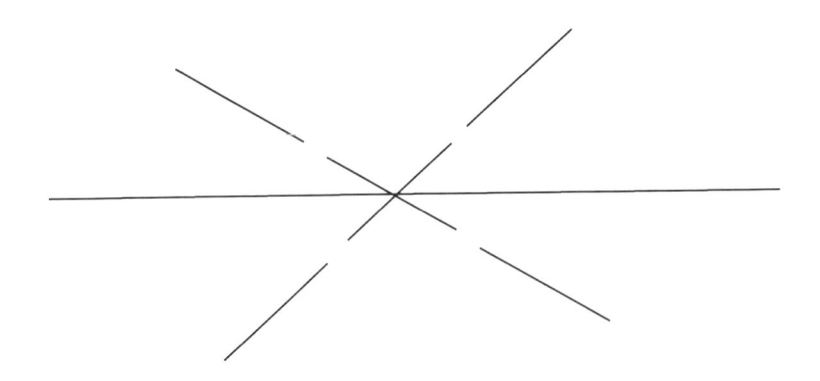

We have that dotted X on that straight line to remind us that life is not built on a level. Then, what is life built on?

INCLINE

Life is built on an incline. Because of that incline, we only have two choices. We are either learning and growing or slipping. Because of the incline, eventually the slip will turn into a slide, a massive slide. Therefore, we cannot stand still. We cannot stay even. Life is a dynamic experience, and we cannot stand still. Since the purpose of life is movement, we want to continue to move onward, upward, and forward. This means each second of each day - RIGHT NOW - we have two choices:

GETTING BETTER AND BETTER OR **GETTING WORSE AND WORSE**

How are we getting better and better or worse and worse?

**STEP BY STEP
BIT BY BIT
LITTLE BY LITTLE
OR A
LITTLE AT A TIME**

The following clarifies how we can be a beacon of light by being "hungry to share" in numerous minute ways.

Sharing

There isn't much that I can do, but I can share my bread with you, and sometimes share a sorrow, too — as on our way we go.

There isn't much that I can do, but I can set an hour with you, and I can share a joke with you, and sometimes share reverses, too — as on our way we go.

There isn't much I can do, but I can share my flowers with you, and I can share my books with you and sometimes share your burdens, too — as on our way we go.

There isn't much that I can do, but I can share my hopes with you, and I can share my fears with you, and sometimes shed some tears with you — as on our way we go.

There isn't much that I can do, but I can share my friends with you, and I can share my life with you, and oftentimes share a prayer with you — as on our way we go.
Author Unknown[1]

      Finally, one of my primary daily goals is to remain humble all the time, not simply to impress other people or to get my own way. We could be working on this one goal (being humble with our family, friends, relatives, neighbors, telephone operators, truck drivers, waiters, and waitresses) our entire lives and never arrive, but we can be on the "grow." One of the greatest things in life is to be learning to be an authentic, sincere, and humble human being. Truly, it is exciting to meet/become this type of person, because a real person in today's world stands out like a sore thumb, but a sore thumb in a positive way. We have many false ideas about humility, incorrectly associating it with being:

- soft
- passive
- weak, or
- wimpish

Humility has nothing to do with these because you can be humble and still be:

- brave
- strong
- smart, and
- assertive (where you politely but firmly stick up for your rights)

By remaining happy, hungry, and humble, I hope to leave my unique positive thumbprint (daily in small but powerful ways) and improve the world as it is depicted in the following:

The Story of the Oyster
-Anonymous

There once was an oyster whose story I tell who found that sand got under its shell.
Just one little grain, but it gave such pain,

For oysters have feelings although they are so
plain. Now, did it berate the workings of fate
which
had led to such a deplorable state?
Did it curse the government, call for an election
Or cry that the sea should have given
protection?
No, as it lay on the ocean shelf, it said to itself
"If I cannot remove it, I'll try to improve on it."
So the years rolled by as years always do and it
came to its ultimate destiny -oyster stew.
Now the small grain of sand which bothered it so,
was a beautiful pearl, translucent aglow!
This tale has a moral-for isn't it grand what an
oyster can do with a morsel of sand?
What could we do if we'd only begin with all
things that get under our skin?[2]

Why not, as the oyster did, turn our irritations into pearls, our scars into stars, and our wounds into wisdom?

FOOD FOR THOUGHT

"Never look down on anybody unless you are helping them up."
Jesse Jackson

"Humility is really important because it keeps you fresh and new."
Steven Tyler

"Humility is nothing but truth and pride is nothing but lying."
St. Vincent de Paul

"Humility is having awe for being a speck in an infinite universe rather than seeing yourself as the center of it."
Judith Orloff

"True knowledge exists in knowing that you know nothing."
Socrates

"Humility is not thinking less of yourself; it's thinking of yourself less."
C. S. Lewis

"Mastery begins with humility."
  Robin Sharma

"The biggest challenge after success is shutting up about it."
Criss Jami

"A great man is always willing to be little."
Ralph Waldo Emerson

"Humility is trying your best to surmount self-doubts, even if someone gets what you deserve or outdoes you."
Judith Orloff

"Think lightly of yourself and deeply of the world."
  Miyamoto Musashi

"Humility will open more doors than arrogance ever will."
     Zig Ziglar

"Let us be grateful to people who make us happy."
Marcel Proust

MYTH #3:

BEING GRATEFUL FOR WHAT WE HAVE IS NOT ONLY THE KEY TO SUCCESS BUT ALSO OUR KEY TO INNER PEACE.

REALITY:
WE NEED TO EXPAND OUR CONCEPTS ABOUT GRATITUDE.

Being grateful for what we have is not only the key to our success but also to our inner peace. The quickest, easiest, and most enjoyable way to get from where you are to where you want to be is to focus on each moment in awe with gratitude. Why?

"What you focus on, expands."- Esther Jno-Charles

Therefore, if you are grateful and focus on your blessings, you will earn additional blessings. You can make or break any day of your life by telling yourself all of the good news that you can, as soon as you get up each morning.

However, we must expand our definition of gratefulness to include things which could have happened to us but did not. After scrutinizing the following list, please put a checkmark by each item that applies to you, now or in your past:

- Tinnitus
- Syncope
- Peripheral neuropathy
- Edema in both feet
- Carpal tunnel in both wrists
- Ulnary nerve problems in both arms
- Spinal stenosis in cervical spine
- Over six operations

- Nervous breakdown
- Business fiascoes
- Death of a child
- Almost run over by a car
- Stubborn hypertension
- Hypothyroidism
- Spinal challenges
- Generalized anxiety and panic attacks in 2011
- Several biopsies
- Generalized anxiety, panic attacks, and agoraphobia in 2014
- Osteopenia
- Keratoconus
- Stent (right renal artery)

All the above have been a part of my history, and many of them are still challenges to me. Yet, I consider myself to be blessed and healthy. You might analyze that list and consider all of them to be "negatives."

However, in every situation, you will find positives along with negatives, but what do you choose to focus on? Let us use my almost being hit by a car as a prime example of this concept (finding positives along with negatives in each situation). On March 1, 2019, I went for a walk outside. About a block away from my house, I encountered a temporary loss of consciousness (syncope) and passed out right in the middle of a street. I injured my tailbone, spine, hit the back of my head, and then somehow managed to hit my left shoulder, and left thumb. A car was approaching but fortunately saw me and stopped a few feet in front of me. What can I be grateful for in this situation - the things that could have happened to me, but did not?

- The car running over me
- Broken bones
- Fractures
- Concussion

- Becoming a paraplegic

If this incident would have happened while I was driving, I could have inadvertently killed or marred other innocent people.

The third way (in addition to being grateful for our blessings and the things that could have happened to us but didn't) we should expand our definition of gratitude is to be cognizant that some of our blessings can be attributed to the prayers of other people on our behalf.

To illustrate, let me share with you the story of a spiritual warrior, my good friend, Jim Korzi who passed away on March 13, 2019. I was both honored and humbled, mainly humbled, to offer the following eulogy in honor of him.

I am one of Jim's numerous (That is "numerous" with a capital "N"!) friends. Actually, throughout the years, Jim, Dwight Kauffman, Joe

Oresko *(who- rather than asking what he could do to help- immediately volunteered to be one of Jim's primary caregivers, which he did with the utmost love possible until Jim's dying day)* and I bonded, and they became the brothers that I never had. I never wanted to take their everlasting friendship for granted, and I also wanted them to know how much I deeply appreciated their friendships, so I constantly wrote them notes. I would usually end with the following quotation by Voltaire: **"Friends, such as you, should be preferred to kings."** I share with you the following story because it clearly exemplifies one of Jim's constant daily prayers.

Two best friends went on a voyage together. The ship wrecked and they were the only survivors. Being excellent swimmers, they were able to swim safely to a nearby island.

They knew that they were in deep trouble and their only recourse was to turn to God. However, they decided to test the power of each other's prayers. One man went to the left side of the island and prayed for food. The next day, a fruit tree appeared with edible fruit. Nothing appeared on the other side of the island. Next the man on the left-hand side was lonely and prayed for a wife. Soon, another ship wrecked and a lovely woman swam to his side of the island. Again, nothing took place on the other side of the island. Next the man on the left prayed for more food, clothes, and even a house, and he got all of these but "ZILCH" on the other side of the island. Finally, the man on the left side became homesick and prayed to go home. The next day, a ship docked on his side of the island. He had no qualms about leaving his friend on the island, because he had become arrogant assuming that all his prayers had been answered, but none of his friend's prayers had been answered. However, as he was about to leave, a voice, from the heavens, demanded to know why he was not taking his friend with him. Sarcastically, he pointed out that his friend was a "LOSER," because none of his prayers had been answered. Again, the voice boomed but stipulated that his friend's prayers had been answered. Befuddled, he asked what the prayer was and was informed his prayer was, that "all of your prayers would be answered."[1]

Guess what Jim's constant daily prayer was:

"Lord, please send me all the health challenges and spare all my loved ones." What follows are

some of the health challenges that Jim heroically endured, like the spiritual warrior that he was until his dying day:
- Open heart surgery
- Two hip replacements
- Right leg amputated right beneath the knee
- Prostate cancer
- Radiation treatments
- Spinal stenosis
- Cataract surgeries
- Balance problems

Is that not the closest anyone can come to unconditional love here on this earth?

In 2018, I attended a seminar on **"Chronic Pain Management,"** and the facilitator, a man, pointed out that on a scale of one to ten (ten being the most severe pain) a ten to a woman would be childbirth, but to a man it would be a common cold. When it comes to handling health challenges, personally I am a wimp, but Jim was a "RARE BIRD" (saying this with the utmost respect possible) in his tenacious ability to tolerate pain. As Jim matured, he focused on his faith, family, and friends, understanding that real living is all about relationships. Because of the traits previously mentioned, I consider Jim to be a **HERO** in the highest sense possible. Mary, his angelic wife, is also to be commended for the love, time, effort, and sacrifices that she lovingly exhibited toward him until he passed. Now, WWJD has a twofold meaning for me:

- "What would Jesus do?" and
- "What would Jim (and Mary) do?"[2]

The final, and the most important, way that we should amplify our explication of gratitude is to focus on the "BLESSER"(as Jim did daily by saying his prayers and reciting the Rosary) and not simply our blessings. If we merely focus on our blessings, other people might become forlorn, if they feel that they did not receive as many blessings as we did. However, we all have the same "BLESSER!"[3] This was distinctly brought home to me in an exhilarating CD by Charles Jones entitled ***"It's all about Jesus,"*** where he includes his favorite prayer:

Dear Lord, if I can be of most use by being of no use, then let me be learning to be of no use if that's the way I can be of most use. But please, Lord, never let my usefulness be the basis of my joy. Let my joy always be His joy, Himself, Christ in me… plus nothing.[4]

Len LaPlaca's TWO FAVORITE PRAYERS:

I rest silently before you, Lord, waiting for you to rescue me, since salvation comes from you alone. Jesus, you are my •ROCK •RESCUER •REFUGE• REDEEMER •DEFENSE •STRENGTH •FORTRESS •PROTECTION•GUIDE and my• LIGHT. I turn all my thoughts over to the Holy Spirit. I am now at peace (say this in the morning before I get out of bed).

SECOND PRAYER(said in the morning but also throughout the day when I want additional energy) *Jesus, please allow the Holy Spirit to enter me NOW and infuse me with a tremendous amount of positive energy, love, wisdom and unconditional happiness, so that I can be the best person I can be, the best Christian that I can be, helping people with no strings attached until my dying day. I turn all my thoughts over to the Holy Spirit. I am now at peace. This, I ask in your name, Jesus. Amen.*

To me, the highest form of gratitude is constantly repeating the three most powerful words in the English language: THANK YOU JESUS! By putting the emphasis on Him, you will reap many benefits such as humility, leaving no space for complaining or any type of negativity and putting the focus where it belongs - on God.

FOOD FOR THOUGHT

"Let gratitude be like the sun to your flower. Keep your face always turned toward its light."
Leah D. Schade

"I would maintain that thanks are the highest form of thought and that gratitude is happiness doubled by wonder."
Gilbert K Chesterson

"Thank you is the best prayer that anyone could say… say that one a lot."
Alice Walker

"Be thankful for what you have; you'll end up having more. If you concentrate on what you don't have, you will never ever have enough."
Oprah Winfrey

"Reflect upon your present blessings, of which every man has plenty; not on your past misfortunes, of which all men have some."
Charles Dickens

After being robbed, Mathew Henry, who lived in the eighteenth century, wrote the following in his diary: ***"Let me be thankful first because I was never robbed before; second, although they took my purse, they did not take my life; third, because although they took my all it was not much; and fourth, because it was I who was robbed, not I who robbed."***

> "To retire is to die."
> **Pablo Casals**

MYTH #4:
IF YOU CAN'T DO IT WELL, DON'T DO IT AT ALL.
REALITY:
DO IT OVER POORLY ENOUGH TIMES UNTIL YOU CAN DO IT WELL.

If you truly believe this myth, you will never invent your own lightbulb, or anything else of value because you will not be willing to endure the effort, time, failures, and sacrifices that are vital in creating it.

We shall use public speaking as an example since stage fright has always ranked in the top 50 of the greatest fears of Americans. What is the common denominator among Demosthenes, Thomas Jefferson, Abraham Lincoln, and Gandhi - their fear of public speaking! They overcame their fear of stage fright by doing it over and over, poorly, enough times until they could do it well. To clarify, Demosthenes was born in Athens, Greece in 384 BC. Because of his body shape, he did not participate in sports. In addition to his unbecoming demeanor, occasionally he stammered and could not pronounce the letter "r." This stuttering was amplified by a shortness of breath, possibly asthma, which enabled him to speak only a few words at a time. Naturally, this made him very embarrassed to speak in public again.

After being laughed at by an audience, he was followed home by a man (One person can make a positive difference, and that person can be you!) who was in the audience, and he started coaching him on how to overcome his speech challenges.

Demosthenes developed a daily protocol to become an outstanding speaker. This became his DMI (DEEP MOTIVATING INTEREST) which is a combination of two factors:

1. Goal Setting and
2. The drive, desire, determination, and guts to arrive at those goals.

As a starting point, he went into semi-hiding, so he could focus on practicing his speeches out loud. Also, he occasionally rehearsed speaking before a large mirror. Not only did he recite his speeches out loud, but he also put pebbles into his mouth. This forced him to articulate, slow down while speaking, and pause for different punctuation marks. As he felt he was improving, he would remove a few pebbles from his mouth at a time. After he removed all of them, he no longer stammered or stuttered, and he had the beginning of a natural flow to his speaking. This enabled him to enunciate clearly what he had said, instead of rushing through what he was stipulating. To increase his lung capacity, he not only jogged on the beach, but also he ran up hills and on the stairs of famous Greek buildings.

One of the keys to the success of Demosthenes as a gifted orator was not simply to drill but to practice "correctly." He was able to do this because he was receptive, enabling him to collaborate and learn from others. Remember the man mentioned earlier who stepped in to lend a hand and tutor him. What did Demosthenes do to improve?
Daily he:
- PRACTICED CORRECTLY
- PRACTICED CORRECTLY AND PRACTICED CORRECTLY EVEN MORE!

The key word is not practice but proper practice. Using my own life as an example since I love basketball, one of my goals (at the tender age of 104) is to be assisted on a basketball court, and I would consistently shoot my unorthodox left-handed hook shot (developed this so I would not be "jammed" by the much taller players when I drove to the basket), until I made a basket. After accomplishing this goal, then I would die peacefully on the basketball court.

Imagine that I wanted to excel at basketball. Therefore, daily I would practice a minimum of five hours. Would this lead to my perfection as a basketball player? The answer is not simply "no" but an emphatic "no!"

Suppose that every day I launched hook shots from half-court for five hours. This could have an adverse effect on improving my basketball skills in numerous ways. First, I am squandering valuable time. Next, frustration might set in because I might not be improving, even though I am dedicating much time to this goal.

Finally, negative habit patterns might be arduous to eradicate, as I attempt to improve. "Practice makes perfect" is a fallacy. The reality is that practice makes permanent sometimes for better but quite often for worse. Proper or perfect practice makes perfect.

This myth (If you can't do it well, don't do it at all) might hamper your development the most when you are attempting to move successfully out of your comfort zone. Your comfort zone is how you see yourself or how others see you. While in your comfort zone, you have the same thoughts, feelings, ideas, and behaviors. A comfort zone is a wonderful place to be because it is where you learn what works for you, your haven, and where you discover your unique personality. Most people like what is familiar to them and devalue the strange, different, and foreign. Because what you daily do in your comfort zone is familiar to you, these are done with ease. Therefore, you can relax, enjoy yourself, and position yourself for future growth. Even though you can still try new things and evolve while still in your comfort zone, your comfort zone might blind you with the luxuries and the satisfaction which might stall your growth.

To avert each day being Groundhog Day while staying in your comfort zone, experiment with small changes, and leave your comfort zone because you want to rather than trying to prove to other people that you can handle major changes.

Knowing that - IF YOU CAN'T DO IT WELL, DON'T DO IT AT ALL! - is a myth will be advantageous to you, if you want to venture successfully out of your comfort zone. While moving astutely out of our comfort zones, we can learn more skills, achieve our goals, and discover more opportunities. In order to move successfully out of our comfort zones, we need to enhance/develop new traits and be aware of four things. "What we don't know will hurt us!"

Doctor Bruce Larson was given a fellowship to travel all over the world for a specific period of time in an attempt to answer the following question:
"What factors lead to an increase in the mental health of people?"
Also, the opposite of the same coin:
"What factors lead to a decrease in mental health and a corresponding increase in mental illness?"

After years of exhaustive study, Doctor Larson came up with one word, a four - letter word! If you incorporate this word into your life, this will lead to an increase in your mental health, an increase in your self - respect. Why? Now, you know that you can successfully meet challenges and experiences. This will lead to your trusting yourself even more than in the past when confronting future challenges. However, if you delete this word from your life, this will lead to a decrease in your mental health, and a decrease in your self - respect. No, the four letter word is not love, care, give, or hope, but the four letter word is **RISK**. Stepping out of the bounds of your comfort zone is a risk. We are not advocating your becoming a foolish risk-taker and jumping out of your comfort zone at the drop of a hat, especially moving from one job/activity to the other, but instead encouraging you to be a sensible calculated risk-taker. One of the fringe benefits of doing this is that you get to know yourself better, learning what you relish as well as what you don't savor doing.

What are the four things that you must be aware of, while moving out of your comfort zone?

To begin with, moving out of your comfort zone is uncomfortable, so why not *choose* when you enter this period of discomfort? You have more ascendency by choosing. For example, since I am 79 and JoAnn, my wife, is 71, would it not be prudent for us now to begin to look into moving to a retirement community rather than be dictated by a death or a health crisis or domination by a family member? By doing this, we are enthusiastically learning to accept the challenge of change. You now understand that it is normal, natural, and to be expected when you go through this first stage that you will either look or feel awkward, clumsy, and/or uncomfortable. The startling, good news is that your creativity is stimulated because you are endeavoring novel things or even seeing or doing new things. Because of the novelty of the event, you will tend to heighten not only your concentration but also your focus. Next, as you move out of your comfort zone, never criticize yourself, and thirdly, never let anyone else criticize you. If you denounce yourself or allow anyone to condemn you, the focus is on negativity. Since you are focusing on negatives, you will earn additional gloom in your life. Why? "What you focus on, expands." Finally, praise the movement, no matter how awkward that movement might be. Even though we might be challenged and frightened when moving out of our comfort zones, we will also be learning and growing which will stimulate us and give us additional confidence. This is indeed a risk worth taking!

    What can we learn not only from the life of Demosthenes but also others who have overcome their fears? First, there are no substitutes for being assiduous and deliberately practicing, that is practicing correctly. What enabled him to practice correctly was his receptivity not only to mentors but also dissident methods, such as putting pebbles in his mouth and jogging.

Today, you have numerous modern techniques and programs that, if you implement properly, can reduce years on your learning curve. If you remain receptive, as Demosthenes did, you can not only possibly overcome your fears but also in a shorter time because of the things that are available today.

FOOD FOR THOUGHT

Risk

To laugh is to risk appearing the fool.

Laugh anyway.

To weep is to risk appearing sentimental.

Weep anyway.

To reach out for another is to risk involvement.

Get involved anyway.

To expose feelings is to risk exposing your true self.

Be vulnerable anyway.

To place your ideas and dreams before the crowd is to

risk their loss.

Present your ideas anyway.

To love is to risk not being loved in return.

Love anyway.

To hope is to risk despair.

Hope anyway.

To try is to risk failure.

Try anyway.

To live is to risk dying.

Live anyway.   **– Anonymous**

"God never takes anything from us without giving us something greater in return."

Old Proverb

MYTH #5:
WE NEED TO TAKE CONTROL OF OUR LIVES.

REALITY:
CONTROL IS A MYTH.

In the past, you did not have control. Presently, you do not have control. In the future, you will not have control. However, you are in control of planning properly for what happens, what you think, your ability to focus, how generous and grateful you are, and choosing how to respond in the most effective manner possible to what has just happened. The key word is not planning but flexible planning which means that whatever might go wrong will go wrong, and it will go wrong at the wrong time. This is a part of my plan that my plan might go wrong. Therefore, I have another plan waiting in the wings.

Also, you get to choose how to respond to each event. Could each event that you ever encounter be neutral, and how you choose to respond will determine the unique outcome for you?

To illustrate that your response (which you have total control over) is more important than the event, the following story is taken from the book, *The DNA of Success* by Jack M. Zufelt.

Michael Dowling was the president of one of the largest banks in St. Paul. When World War One broke out he asked for a leave of absence because he wanted to go to Europe and talk to the soldiers, especially the wounded ones. On one occasion, he was speaking in a mammoth hotel in London and had before him many wounded soldiers, some in wheelchairs, others lying on cots, and some with missing arms, legs, eyes, and hands. Steps separated Michael Dowling, who was located in the mezzanine, from the soldiers who were located in the lobby area. When he started to speak, he minimized their wounds and emphasized that they had no grounds for complaints and all would work out for them. Therefore, there should be no major concerns in their minds. The soldiers got really perturbed with him, since that message did not set well with them. So, they started to boo him boisterously and vehemently. How dare he come all the way over to Europe to tell them that their wounds did not affect their lives negatively? They knew better. In the middle of the booing, Michael Dowling walked down a few of the steps while telling them how fortunate they are. Then, he sat down on one of the steps and took off his right leg. The booing persisted but definitely not as loudly. When he took off his left leg, the booing stopped. By the time he had arrived at the bottom of the steps, he had taken off his right arm, and slipped off his left hand. There he sat, the shambles of a man, telling them to focus on what they had, not on what was missing.[1]

Michael Dowling did make a positive difference in the lives of those wounded soldiers only because of his unique response to a so-called horrific event when he was 14 years old. At that age, he was in the back of a wagon being driven by his parents. Because of a dire blizzard, he was knocked unconscious, unbeknown to his parents. Before his parents could find him, he was severely frost-bitten. He was taken to a hospital and the following was done:

- Right leg amputated almost to the hip
- Left leg amputated above the knee
- Amputated his right arm
- Amputated his left hand

However, Michael Dowling eventually became the president of one of the largest banks in the St. Paul area, married, and was the father of five children.[2]

Consider this story of a one - armed ten-year-old boy to clarify even further the importance of your PRA (Positive Response Attitude). This narration (could be fictional) is about a young boy who lost his left arm in a horrific car accident. This ten-year-old boy became depressed because he could no longer remain involved in a variety of activities, especially sports which he relished. He became more and more isolated from everything and everyone.

Therefore, his comfort zone became smaller and smaller, as he became more and more isolated.

His mother, at her wit's end because of her concern for her son, suggested different activities for her son to become involved so that his confidence would increase. Unfortunately, he refused all her ideas. However, when one of his friends began taking judo lessons, he reluctantly agreed to go with him. Soon he began taking lessons from an elderly astute Japanese master. Even though the boy was doing well, he could not fathom why the master had taught him only one move. He would see the other students learning different techniques and asked the master why he wasn't learning anything else. The master always calmly replied just to focus on the one technique that he was teaching him. The master emphasized not only to keep practicing but also doing it with the utmost pride possible and to maintain a positive mental attitude.

Several months later, the Sensei took the boy to his first tournament, which happened to be the state Judo championship. Needless to say, the young boy was petrified. Would you believe that stage fright applies to everyone to whom performance really matters? Stage fright has many positive aspects, since it means that you care - really care - not taking your responsibilities too lightly, have a healthy respect for the opposition, and are utilizing all of your God - given talents.

When the first match began, the one-armed boy grabbed his opponent and easily flipped him to the ground for an instant win. This shocked not only the spectators but also the one-armed boy. Even though the second round was arduous, the one-armed boy pulled off the only technique that he knew and won.

After amazingly winning the third and fourth rounds in the same way, he now found himself facing an opponent, who had won this tournament for three straight years. This adversary was bigger, tougher, and stronger than anyone he had ever encountered.

On paper, the young boy was overmatched, but things are seldom what they appear to be. Why?

"Skim milk often masquerades as cream."
W.S. Gilbert

Having compassion for the one-armed boy, not only the referee but also the organizers of the tournament implored the master to withdraw his student.

To the dismay of everyone concerned, the master adamantly insisted that they would fight. As the match progressed, the one-armed boy appeared to be overmatched and in jeopardy of getting seriously marred. Concerned that the boy might get hurt, the referee called a time out and was about to stop the match, but the Sensei intervened and insisted that the match should continue.

After the match resumed, his opponent made a critical mistake, and instantly the boy used his move to pin him. The boy had won not only the match but also the tournament. Now, he was the reigning champion. On the drive home, the young boy, being totally baffled, asked his teacher if they let him win, because he had only one arm. He knew that his opponents mastered hundreds of techniques, but he was aware of only one.

However, his teacher made it crystal clear that he had won fair and square. The master specified that he had won for two primary reasons. He won because he had almost mastered one of the most difficult and devastating techniques in Judo.

Secondly, there is only one known way to defend against that throw and that is to grab the left arm.[3]

Notice how the one-armed boy's response to the event (horrendous accident resulting in the loss of his left arm) led to the unusual outcome for him - becoming the state Judo champion. Could each event that you ever encounter be neutral and how you choose to respond (have total control over this) to the event will determine the extraordinary outcome for you?

Finally, "inspiring" is a word to describe the responses of Susan Cook to her lifelong ordeal with MS. Even though I did not personally know this audacious lady, Pam Carls (author of The Winners' Journal and the Christian Winners' Journal-269-342-8547 Dr. John and Pam Carls) not only introduced me to Susan's ABCs of Little Life Lessons but also went one step further and got permission from her gracious family to allow me to include it in my book. Susan truly was an "Angel on wheels," not allowing her wheelchair to slow her down or becoming involved in a continuous self-pity party, but instead chose to respond by focusing on specific ways to help others. With the utmost pride possible but also with great humility, I now share with you Susan's alphabet ABCs of Little Life Lessons.

ABC's of Little Life Lessons
By Susan Cook

A

School is an ATTITUDE, not always a classroom.

We are learning new information each day.

"A"- is for AHH

(that's Attitude Adjustment Hour)

A time to reflect each day:

Where have I been?

Where am I now?

Where am I going?

Nurture an Attitude of Gratitude.

B

BLOOM where you are planted

C

COMMUNICATION and COURAGE

Fine tune your Christian Character each day.

D

DAILY DEVOTION

What a way to begin each morning!

It gives a boost to each day

and keeps your thoughts and deeds on track.

Daily devotions help each day develop beautifully.

E

ENTHUSIASM

This word comes from the Greek word Enthus,

meaning "God Within."

How could we want for more?

Enthusiasm can't be equaled by any other quality.

F

FAITH

Christian Faith is:

assuring,

insuring,

enduring.

Our spiritual life in action!

Faith, my friend, will see you through.

G

GOD

Give glory to God for his goodness.

God's Goodness is all around.

H

Hold on! Hang in there!

Let sincere Hugs be the mortar

between you and humanity.

I

INSPIRATION

"I" is in the middle when you are Inspired or

Inspiring.

J

WWJD

What would JESUS do?

Journaling.

Write 3 things down you are grateful for each day.

K

Kindness

Daily, all year through.

An act of Kindness benefits both giver and receiver.

L

LOVE & LAUGHTER

Make a long life!

Love and Laughter sure lighten the load.

M

MIRACLES

Happen to those who believe.

Millions of Miracles happen every day!

Look for them!

N

NEIGHBORS

Become a friend to your neighbor today!

Neighbors are so nice!

Learn 2 new facts about yours.

O

OPPORTUNITIES

Opportunities are abundant, if we just catch hold.

Send a note,

call a friend, meet someone new.

P

PEACE and PATRIOTISM

should go hand in hand, but will take many public and

private prayers worldwide to accomplish.

PRAYER

Such a gift, opportunity, freedom, Privilege and source

of Peace!

Q

QUALITY

Quality time is very achievable, if we quizzically search ourselves as if this was our last day on Earth. Put Quality into the Quantity of time we have on this earth.

R

RESPECT

Reflect a Radiance of Respect?

Of course you can!

Develop an Armor of Self-Respect.

Demonstrate a rapport of Respect with others.

Reflect the best qualities you received

From your relatives before you.

S

SMILE

A Sincere Smile;

The world can always use more!

The least expensive gift you can give,

The most generous gift others can receive!

T

TRUTHFUL

TRUSTWORTHY

THOUGHTFUL

What we want most in others, and they want most in us.

U

UNITY

UNITED

UNIVERSAL

UNDERSTANDING

All starting with the community,

The nation our world.

Each beginning with "U."

Understanding; first ourselves, then

our neighbors, our country and our world

To be United and live in peace and

Unity with ALL people.

V

VISION

Let others Visually View your Values;

not just in Voice but through Vitality and Virtue,

and as you Vow to Volunteer and

exercise your privilege to Vote.

W

WE

Such a small word, yet so powerful

when all of us stand tall for united goals

WISDOM

Wisdom is a gift we each have earned when

mixed with Wit, which is more easily learned.

Watch for opportunity to Witness in Wholesome talk.

Let both Wisdom and Wit shine through each day as we go forth in our daily Walk,

giving Worship and praises.

X

(Please note that we are "ignoring" the letter "e" when making our "X" words.)

First comes exciting, as our life should be.

Next is example, be a good one to see.

Then extra, as in go the extra mile to help another person, to bring forth a smile!

Y

YOU

You are in charge of just one person, Yourself.

You can say Yes.

YES

Say "Yes" when a helping hand is

needed or

someone needs a friend.

It is so good for "You",

and especially for those you help!

"Yield" not to temptation -

like an extra piece of dessert, or just sitting a

spell instead of taking a healthy walk.

"Youthful" attitude will remain if "You" partner

with

a young person.

Z

Be a bit "Zany"

It's fun to have fun!

Be a little "Zealous"

That's enthusiastic!

Be "Zippy" and "zoè tic"

Lively, alert & dynamic!

Put "Zest" in all you do!

You will reach "Zenith",

The very top of what's good for you![4]

FOOD FOR THOUGHT
LIFE INSURANCE

Let me tell you of the insurance
That I have on my life.

Just knowing that I have it
Has eased all stress and strife.

The Salesman was a Master
of the well-known "soft sell."

I listened quite reluctantly
Though my
doubts He'd soon dispel.

He said I'd be insured
For the rest of my days.

But the strangest part of all
Is how this insurance pays.

For now, and when I leave this earth,
All benefits are paid to ME!

It is wonderful to know
I'll be the beneficiary.

For the Salesman was Jesus
A man with true endurance.

Who gave everything I need
When he gave me life insurance.
He even paid the premiums
And believe me, they were high!

He hung in shame for me
Upon a cross to die.

I'll let you read the policy
If you still have any doubt.

It's written in the Bible
I'll let you search it out.

You can read the fine print
Checking out the clauses.

The Salesman will gladly call
Without any pauses.

Is there any question?
You think this insurance odd?

Make this consideration
The guarantor is God![5]

Susan Cook

"If we all did the things we are capable of, we would astound ourselves."
Thomas Edison

MYTH #6:

THE TRUTH WILL SET YOU FREE.

REALITY:

YOUR TRUTH ABOUT YOURSELF IS OFTEN FALSE.

    A personal philosophy is apt because it guides, leads, and directs you on a daily basis. Since life is movement, your radically distinctive personal philosophy will help you to continue to move onward, upward, and forward. By focusing on the individual aspects of your personal philosophy, you will be centering on the positive attributes - while not waging a war against the negatives of the world but simply ignoring them - that you deem to be significant. By using your personal philosophy as your day-by-day center of attraction you will be "attracting" more of these positive traits. Why? "What you focus on, expands."

My personal philosophy is:
With enthusiasm I always attempt to give more than I take, I have an attitude of gratitude, and daily I live the truth about myself.

The last four letters **(IASM)** in the word enthusiasm stand for:

I AM SOLD ON MYSELF

Before you can be sold on yourself and do the best you can with what you have got, you must understand the truth about yourself, since your truth about yourself is often false. So, we want to answer this permeating question:

What is the truth about you?

The following ten statements sagaciously summarize the truth about you.
You are you!

Here we are emphasizing your unearthing, your authentic you. To illustrate, a Thai monastery, many centuries ago, was the home of a mammoth and picturesque statue of Buddha, all golden. The Burmese army was about to invade this area and the monks wanted to protect the statue from pillage, but they could not move it to safe territory, because they were not only frail but also elderly. So, they covered the statue with plastered clay, eight to twelve inches thick. Even though we say, "Trickery won't do the trick," in this case the trick worked, and the warlords deemed the statue to be worthless, but all the monks were slaughtered in the attack. Fast forward to 1957 when the monastery was being relocated by a group of monks. A crane was arranged to carry the "clay" statue, but it was much heavier than anticipated, and one of the monks noticed a large crack in the clay. When the statue was diligently inspected with the help of a little chiseling, a solid gold statue of infinite worth was discovered.[1]

Your natural state (THE REAL YOU) is the Golden Buddha, but have you allowed, either consciously or unconsciously, yourself to get covered in layer upon layer of clay? Layers of clay have been added by our culture, parents, peer group pressure, our educational system, the mass media of communication, and even organized religion. If we delete these layers of clay, we will return to our own natural state, our own Golden Buddha. Visualize yourself being Wonder Woman or Superman. We get to choose our capes - velcro or teflon. If we choose a velcro cape, all the negativities that are thrown our way will adhere to us, and, eventually, we will be overwhelmed by them, thus draining our natural energy and strength. However, if we choose a teflon cape because of its nonstick nature, all negativities will not cling to us. Not only is teflon completely resistant to water, but we can also use our capes to resist and refuse negativities and simply let them "slide off" and tremendously lighten our burdens. "You are you" might appear to be a mundane statement, but we have a certain number of Americans who don't comprehend this concept, therefore simply following the crowd or the leader. Your goal should not be a different you but the best rendition of yourself that you can be. If you don't appreciate your authentic self, you might mistakenly become a facsimile, a carbon copy of other people.

However, as Emerson says, "Imitation is suicide," and as Lucretius, an ancient Latin writer exclaimed; "What is one man's meat is another man's poison." If you live a hundred lifetimes, you still will not utilize all your potential. That is how powerful you really are, when you are your authentic self! Oscar Wilde stated, "Be yourself, everyone else is already taken." You are then being true to yourself, and you will be living by a code of morals and values. Could this possibly be the best piece of advice that anyone can give you?

You are not inferior! You have made mistakes, but you personally are not a mistake. If you continue to grow (THE PURPOSE OF LIFE), you will make additional mistakes. Making mistakes is a natural and important part of your development. When we minimize our power and maximize the positive attributes of others, the result is a feeling of inferiority. Most of us make these two mistakes when it comes to intelligence: overestimating the intelligence of other people and underestimating our own. Rather than constantly focusing on what you deem to be your inferior state, why not focus on the many things you can do better than the people who you consider to be superior to you? One of my favorite quotations is the following by Eleanor Roosevelt, "No one can make you feel inferior without your consent." Do not give anyone permission to do that to you! Each person can excel in something, but no one can excel in everything. Even though we want to be aware of our weaknesses and do our best to amend them, we want to focus on our strong points, which we need not only to recognize but also to strengthen. Using some of these ideas will help you to liberate yourself of your conditioned responses to life.

You are not superior! People who feel superior are divorced from reality because they have an egotistical view of themselves, and thus they think they are more astute, more enterprising, and more prudent than others. In reality, "We are all stupid and clever in a great variety of ways all at the same time." Osho, the Indian spiritual teacher, summed it up perfectly:

"Nobody is superior, nobody is inferior, but nobody is equal either. People are simply unique, incomparable.
You are you. I am I."

If you consider yourself to be a winner, you might become vain, conceited, arrogant, and even lazy. Instead, why not remain humble throughout your entire life?

"If you do not remain humble, you will eventually stumble."- Pastor Rick Warren

Since people who are humble have a healthy dose of self-respect, they do not have to put other people down in their attempts to increase their own self-respect. Humility goes hand in hand with diligence. By doing this, you will continue to develop your talents.

As you began to mature, you then began to understand that inferiority and superiority are opposite sides of the same coin, and that coin is a counterfeit coin. Both complexes - inferiority and superiority - are detrimental to a person because both - in different ways - hamper the development of the person. Because of the fear of rejection, a person who feels inferior will never utilize his tremendous potential. However, since the person with the superiority complex feels superior, he feels he does not need to do anything to improve himself, but the purpose of life is growth. Both complexes can be altered easily since each is a problem of the mind. Because we all are a combination of strengths and struggles, it is imperative to see ourselves with kind eyes. Be gentle with yourself. As Leonard Cohen shares, "Why is there a crack in everything? That is how the light gets through."

You are a child of God! Your identity as a child of God can never be threatened or ever taken away from you. If you focus on being a child of God, this will give you stability in our unstable world. This identity can never be threatened by ANYTHING, and this is startling, good news. God adores you. Can you learn to live with that?

You have been made in the image of God! Superior to any animal, God gave people not only a mind but also emotions, and free will. Since man also was given a Spirit, he has the capacity for not only knowing God but also communicating with Him through prayer, songs of praise, and worship.

You can change your life right now simply by changing your focal point. If you focus on God, He can be your:

Rock

Strength

Guide

Light

Protector

Counselor

Refuge

Rescuer

Redeemer

Defense

Can this be an unbeatable combination - God and you?

When God made you, He threw away the formula. God only made you once. Immediately, He threw away the mold. Why? One of you is enough for Him.

You are unique! When someone specifies that you are unique, consider that to be a compliment, because that indicates that you are engaging. Strive more to be unique!

You are different! Please dispel the notion that different means being weird and or unwanted. Being different, in actuality, means being unique, one of a kind. Dare to be different.

You are unusual! When you accept the notion that you are unusual, this allows you to be true to yourself. This will also enhance your self-esteem, and the whole business of living is to fulfill yourself, to increase your sense of self-respect. If you do not like, appreciate, and respect yourself, you should expect friction and trouble in your life. "You alone are enough," said Maya Angelou, "you have nothing to prove to anybody."

The following story can be found in one of Mabel Katz's wonderful books entitled *"The Easiest Way."*

Once upon a time, in a place that could have been any place, in a time that could have been any time, there was a beautiful garden with apple and orange trees, beautiful roses, all happy and satisfied. Everything was happiness in the garden, expect for a tree that was terribly sad. The poor tree had a problem: It didn't know who it was!

"What you lack is concentration," the apple tree would tell it. "If you really tried, you could have delicious apples. See how easy it is. "Don't listen to him," the rose bush would plead. "It's easier to have roses and look how beautiful we are!" The desperate tree would try everything that they suggested, but since he

couldn't be like the rest, every time he would feel more and more frustrated.

One day an owl arrived at the garden, the wisest of all the birds, and at seeing the desperation of the tree exclaimed, 'Don't worry. Your problem is not that serious. It's the same as that of many human beings on earth! I will give you the solution; Don't dedicate your life to being what others want you to be. Be yourself. Know yourself, and to do that, listen to your inner voice." And having said that, the owl disappeared.

"My inner voice? Be myself? Know myself?" the desperate tree would ask himself, when suddenly he understood. Closing his ears, he opened his heart and finally heard his inner voice telling him "You will never give apples *because you are not an apple tree, and you will not bloom every spring because you are not a rose bush. You are a redwood, and your destiny is to grow tall and majestic: You are here to give shelter to the birds, shade to the travelers, beauty to the countryside! You have a mission! Go for it!" And the tree felt strong and sure of itself and it set itself out to be all that it was meant to be. In this way it quickly filled its space and was admired and respected by everyone. Only then was the garden completely happy.*

As I look around, I ask myself, "How many are redwoods that don't allow themselves to grow? How many are rose bushes that for fear only give thorns? How many orange trees are there that don't know how to bloom?" In life we all have a destiny to fulfill, a space to fill up. Let's not let anything or anyone prevent us from knowing and sharing the marvelous essence of our being.² Wow! Wow! Wow! It cannot be stipulated any better than that. Can it?

FOOD FOR THOUGHT

The POWER of ONE

ONE TREE *can start a forest.*
ONE SMILE *can begin a friendship.*
ONE HAND *can lift a soul.*
ONE ACT can *inspire a movement.*
ONE CANDLE *can wipe out darkness.*
ONE HOPE *can raise our spirits.*
ONE TOUCH *can show you care.*
ONE PERSON *can make a difference…*
Be that **ONE today.**
BJ Gallagher

"If people refuse to look at you in a new light and they can only see you from the mistakes you've made, if they don't realize that you are not your mistakes then they have to go."
Steve Maraboli

MYTH #7:
WE LEARN FROM OUR MISTAKES.

REALITY:
WE LEARN FROM OUR MISTAKES ONLY WHEN WE USE THE SIX-STEP PROCESS.

As a starting point, you should not get bad feelings when you hear the word mistake or when you have made a mistake, because making mistakes is a natural and important part of your development. Very successful people will tell you that they have learned more from their failures or mistakes and have used them as steppingstones, becoming better and not bitter people. By doing this, you can use everything that happens to you to your advantage.

However, when you do make a mistake, use the following six-step process:

1. Admit
2. Analyze
3. Make an honest effort to correct
4. Forget the mistake
5. Keep the lessons
6. Focus on your successes

The first step is to admit immediately your mistake, rather than allowing negativity to enter the scene which would sap your natural energy and strength. Possibly the six most powerful words in the English language are the following:

I
Admit
I
Made
A
Mistake!

This will put you in an elite class, since most people ignore their mistakes or rationalize, use scapegoats, or even attempt to run away from the problem. If you do any of these, the mistake or problem gets bigger, and you get smaller because of a decrease in your self-esteem. However, if you look the problem right in the eyes and instead focus on one of the numerous possible solutions, then the problem gets smaller because of an increase in your self-esteem. By admitting the problem, this frees you from guilt, and not only shows your respect for the other person but also earns you respect.

 After admitting the mistake, the next step is to analyze it. Stop, remain calm, and scrutinize why the mistake was made, so that you don't make it again. Search for flaws in your thinking to pinpoint the cause/causes of your mistake. Why not do additional research and even get advice from your mentors? Why is it so pertinent to remain calm in this process? Each of us has an inner wisdom, but this can only be unlocked when you are calm and relaxed. We learn from our mistakes only when we admit, analyze, and follow the next four steps.

 Next, we need to make an honest effort to correct it. Imagine a landscaper who purchased all his equipment from the same local business firm. However, on one occasion, he was not only treated curtly but also was not given his business discount. He assertively informed the manager, who not only immediately sincerely apologized, but also that same evening took the time - one of his most valuable possessions - to write him a sincere letter of apology and also included a voucher for $100, which could be used at any time in the future. Not only did the manager immediately make an honest effort to rectify the situation, but by going the extra mile, he now had a loyal customer for life.

> *"Customer satisfaction is worthless: customer loyalty is priceless."*
> *-JeffreyGitomer*

When you admit, analyze, and make an honest effort to correct the mistake, you are accepting the responsibility and thus make learning possible. The next step is to forget the mistake. If you focus on the mistake, you will earn additional mistakes, because what you focus on expands. A person is what he remembers. A person is also what he forgets. Sometimes, it is just as important to forget as it is to remember. If you continue to dwell on the mistake, eventually the three Ds will enter the scene:

1. Defeated
2. Disgusted
3. Depressed

In addition, rather than focusing on the mistake, you will focus on the valuable, germane lessons that you learned. If you lose, then learn, and, if you do learn, then you have not lost at all. Being licked is valuable if you learn from it. Always salvage something from every setback.

Finally, when dealing with your mistakes, it would even be more advantageous for you to focus on your successes both now and in the past and even the successes of other people who made similar mistakes and handled them effectively.

When you are audacious enough to share your mistakes and especially your successes in overcoming them, you might be averting others from making the same mistakes that you did. There is nothing wrong with attempting to amend your mistakes, but it is much more useful/effective to focus on what has worked (your past successes), what is working (your present successes) and even the successes of other people in similar fields. Please don't duplicate your mistakes, but instead constantly learn from your successes and the successes of other people. Stop for a moment and learn from those who are doing it correctly. Why?

"School is never out for the pro!"

Contemplate the following since many people view mistakes as totally "bad" parts of their lives, they try to hide them, or forget them, or bury them, and refuse to look at them as anything but intolerable. Why not substitute the word "*experiences*" and transform your mistakes into experiences that helped you grow into the person you are now?

In the engaging book *Life Is Tremendous*, Charles Jones stipulates that God - at birth - gives every person a psychological key ring, and then he gives a law that says,

"Every time you expose yourself to another situation, I'll give you another key of experience for your key ring."[1]

"Unlocked!" | LaPlaca

Lincoln's Key Ring

1. *Failed in Business*
2. *Defeated for Legislature*
3. *Again, Failed in Business*
4. *Sweetheart Died*
5. *Had a Nervous Breakdown*
6. *Defeated for Speaker*
7. *Defeated for Congress*
8. *Defeated for Congress*
9. *Defeated for Senate*
10. *Defeated for Vice-President*
11. *Defeated for Senate*
12. *Elected President*

Let's imagine a psychological key ring for a person, even though only 30 years old, which has many keys on his psychological key ring. How did he earn these - by deliberately exposing himself to a wide variety of experiences, including failures, mistakes, disappointments, headaches, heartaches and put-downs? However, if he did learn from each of these, he earned a key for his key ring. Now, compare this with a 70 year- old who has only a few keys on his ring. Why? Because of a fear of failure or ridicule or stepping out of his comfort zone, the 70-year -old has gained only a few keys on his ring. In the graphic of our psychological key ring above,

11 of the 12 appear to be fiascoes or negatives, but Abraham Lincoln learned from each of them and used these experiences to his advantage to become President of the United States in 1860.

The eloquent Charles Jones (author, executive, humorist, and master of salesmanship) points out in his energizing tapes ("Laughter, Learning, and Leadership"— "Charles 'Tremendous' Jones speaks on leadership") — *("The Seven Laws of Leadership and the Price of Leadership")* that he does not want to be young again. Why? Even though he had more than his share of fun when he was young, overall, he was miserable, because he had only a few keys on his psychological key ring. Deliberately, he exposed himself to a wide variety of situations including failures, disappointments, heartbreaks, setbacks, and headaches. Not only was he learning relevant lessons from each of these and stepping out of his comfort zone (ALL GROWTH OCCURS OUTSIDE YOUR COMFORT ZONE!), but he was also earning keys for his psychological key ring. Soon his key ring began to be filled with experiences, and then he knew how to pick the right key to unlock the situation he faced.

    According to Charles Jones, this is an exciting law because its practice makes things get better and better with added years. As you accumulate experiences, you use these keys (don't need the stamina that you once needed) over and over again.

This law ("Exposure to Experience") is not simply good news but startling, good news because this means you are growing old rather than getting old, if you are diligently practicing the law of exposure to experience. Getting old - not practicing this law - means that you are drifting. Three words characterize the life of any person who is drifting – 1 >>Shallow, 2. >>Cynical, and 3. >> Thankless. Notice the contrast when you are practicing this law, since your life is getting deeper, richer, and fuller. It's exciting to grow old as you practice the law of "Exposure to Experience." [2]

Being 79, this is my favorite sentence! Denis Waitley's quotation relevantly summarizes this section.

"Mistakes are painful when they happen, but years later a collection of mistakes is called experience."

FOOD FOR THOUGHT

"You make mistakes, mistakes don't make you."
Maxwell Maltz

"Mistakes are the growing pains of wisdom."
William Jordan

"We have to make mistakes; it's how we learn compassion for others."
Curtis Sittenfield

"A mistake is only a mistake if you dwell on it. Let go and forgive."
Akiroo Brost

"Smart people learn from their mistakes. But the real sharp ones learn from the mistakes of others."
Brandon Mull

"Do what you love. Know your own bone. Gnaw at it, bury it, unearth it, and gnaw at it still."
-**Henry David Thoreau**

MYTH #8:

SHOW ME A PERSON WHO WORKS, AND I WILL SHOW YOU A SUCCESS.

REALITY:

SHOW ME A PERSON WHO GETS EXCITED ABOUT HER/HIS WORK, AND I WILL SHOW YOU A SUCCESS.

Each of the following quotations illustrates the power or importance of the little-recognized secret of success:

"If you would like to be a power among men, cultivate enthusiasm. People will like you better for it; you will escape the dull routine of a mechanical existence and you will make headway wherever you are. It cannot be otherwise, for this is the human life. Put your soul into your work and not only will you find it pleasanter every hour of the day, but people will believe in you just as they believe in electricity when they get into touch with a dynamo."
Jonathan Ogden Armour

"Without enthusiasm there is no progress in the world."
Woodrow Wilson

"Success consists of going from failure to failure without loss of enthusiasm."
Winston Churchill

"None are so old as those who have outlived enthusiasm."
Henry David Thoreau

"Nothing great was ever achieved without enthusiasm."
Ralph Waldo Emerson

"Enthusiasm is like having two right hands."
Elbert Hubbard

By now, you have discovered that the little recognized secret of success is enthusiasm. The following quotation by Jack London, whose books delighted many people years ago, summarized some of the basic elements of enthusiasm--heat and intelligence:

"I would rather be ashes than dust. I would rather that my spark would burn out in a brilliant blaze than be stifled by dry-rot. I would rather be a superb meteor, every atom of me in magnificent glow, than a sleepy and permanent planet. The proper function of man is to live, not to exist."

The following are the three main fallacies about enthusiasm:

1. Noise
2. Yelling
3. Vigorous action

Enthusiasm has nothing to do with noise, yelling, and vigorous action, especially the type that can be found in political activities, sporting events, and even some types of religious revivals. Why? True enthusiasm is a quiet type of inner confidence!

What is enthusiasm if it has nothing to do with noise, yelling, and/or vigorous action? The following are the key words in different definitions of enthusiasm:

1. Energy
2. Excitement
3. Strong feeling
4. State of caring
5. Strong, rugged mental attitude
6. Throwing your heart over the fence

Enthusiasm is energy, but the key word is not "energy" but "controlled energy." Enthusiasm is excitement, but the key word is not "excitement" but "controlled excitement." Enthusiasm is a strong feeling, but the key words are not "a strong feeling" but "a controlled strong feeling." Why? Enthusiasm can be compared to a fire, but the only kind of fire that counts is a fire under control (your enthusiasm). If you do not have the fire under control, you will burn, and pay the price. Also, enthusiasm is the state of caring, really caring about something. In addition, enthusiasm is a strong, rugged mental attitude that is difficult to maintain but powerful, so powerful. Finally, enthusiasm is throwing your heart over the fence and letting the rest of your body follow.

How can you develop the power of enthusiasm?

1. Use the "as if" principle
2. Discard mistakes
3. Review the good
4. Think positively
5. Learn from your successes
6. Have a goal
7. Have faith

One of the easiest and most effective ways to develop the power of enthusiasm now is to use the "as if" principle. If you want to be successful, courageous, confident, and/or enthusiastic right now, act as if you are already the courageous, confident, successful, and/or enthusiastic person you want to become. You meticulously watch that enthusiastic person and see how he or she:

1. Walks,
2. Talks,
3. Acts,
4. Feels, and
5. Thinks

You incorporate these traits of an enthusiastic person into your own personality, becoming that enthusiastic person you want to be (fake it until you become it).

All kinds of work involve five factors:

1. Detail
2. Monotony
3. Preparation
4. Striving
5. Weariness[1]

When most people hear these words, they get bad feelings (negative). There are no such things as glamorous jobs, as exciting jobs. According to Charles Jones, *"The work involved is not the work itself: the work involved is learning how to get excited about what you are doing right now."*[2] It is easy to get excited (enthusiastic) about someone else's work because right now, you don't have to learn, grow, persevere, plan, struggle, and/or sweat. Also, it is easy to get excited about what you plan to do tomorrow or in the future because right now, you don't have to learn, grow, persevere, plan, struggle, and/or sweat.

How much future will you have (not much) if you are not learning, growing, persevering, struggling, or sweating right now?

Think about the answers to the following three questions:

1. What is your most challenging job?
2. What is your most difficult job?
3. What is your most important job?

Guess what your most challenging, most difficult, and most important job is right now? <u>It is learning how to get excited about what you are doing.</u>

Finally, if we love what we do, everything will flow since we will do it with enthusiasm, and success and wealth will follow, as illustrated in the following story:

A woman went out of her house and noticed three serene elderly men with long white beards sitting in her front yard. She did not recognize them, but they had a spirit of outer joy and inner peace. Even though she did not know them, she felt at ease with them. She said, "I don't think I know you, but you must be hungry. Please come in and have something to eat."

"Is the man of the house home?" they asked.

"No," she said. "He's out."

"Then we cannot go in," they replied.

In the evening, when her husband came home, she told him what had happened. He said, "Do tell them I am home and invite them in."

The woman went out and invited the men in. "We do not go into the house together," they replied.

"Why is that?" She wanted to know.

One of the elderly men explained. "His name is Wealth," he said, pointing to one of his friends. And pointing to another one, he said, "He is

Success, and I am Love." Then he added, "Now go in and discuss with your husband which one of us you want in your home."

The woman went in and told her husband what was said. Her husband was overjoyed. "How nice!" He said. "Since that is the case, let us invite Wealth in. Let him come and fill our home with wealth!"

His wife disagreed. "My dear, why don't we invite in Success?"

Their daughter-in-law was listening from the other corner in the house. She jumped in with her own suggestion, "Would it not be better to invite in Love? Our home will then be filled with love, and peace and joy will follow!"

"Let us heed our daughter-in-law's advice," said the husband to his wife. "Go out and invite Love to be our guest."

The woman went out and asked the three elderly men, "Which one of you is Love? Please come in and be our guest."

Love got up and started walking toward the house. The other two also got up and followed him.

Surprised, the lady asked Wealth and Success, "I only invited Love. Why are you coming in?"

The elderly men replied together, " If you had invited Wealth or Success, the other two of us would have stayed out. But since you invited Love, wherever he goes, we go with him. Wherever there is Love, there is also Wealth and Success!"[3]

Finally, we could summarize this story with the following words: **expose yourself to enthusiasm, or love life and it will love you right back.**

Some people shy away from being enthusiastic because they incorrectly equate it with looking silly, putting on a facade or even being childish.

Personally, I desire energy and have been using the following strategies to be enthusiastic daily.

- Choosing right now to be enthusiastic

  What is the common denominator among happiness, love and enthusiasm? Each of the three is a choice - a number of choices - and not simply a feeling. How can I make enthusasm a daily choice? Make it a day after day practice of focusing on what is going well in my life and getting excited about what I am doing right now.

- Being authentic about the importance that I have placed on enthusiasm

  Hopefully, this will minimize some people of incorrectly assuming that I am putting up a false front and alleviating my fear of looking ludicrous. This will annihilate the "fake it until you make it" element of acquiring enthusiasm,

since continually I will be focusing on the numerous positive elements of being enthusiastic and thus earning more of them.
- Research on how enthusiasm can improve my life

"Some great neurologists have proved that whatever we do with enthusiasm produces only one - tenth the exhaustion of ordinary effort."[4] I will conserve my energy by incorporating enthusiasm, when I have to do anything. Also, if I want to develop the power of enthusiasm into almost anything, I simply dig into it deeper. Imagine that I consider ants to be only pests, especially at a picnic. However, after doing research, I now am amazed when I discover that the ant is one of the world's strongest creatures in relation to its size, carrying 50 times its own body weight. Would you believe that an ant never quits and keeps on trying until it dies? They use the power of synergy by working together to move bigger objects. The bullet ant is said to have the most painful sting in the world. By gathering as much food as possible for the upcoming winter season, the ant is planning ahead. One species of ants (Trap Jaw) holds the record for the fastest movement in the animal kingdom, since it can close its jaws at 140 mph. By doing research and digging into the subject deeper, not only can I develop enthusiasm toward ants but also life, since, usually, the more I am aware about something, the more I will appreciate it and, thus, develop enthusiasm toward it.

- Being a messenger of good news by saying kind words and practicing acts of kindness done deliberately (rather than random acts of kindness) There is a direct correlation between my doing good and my feeling good. By broadcasting good news, I will not only be increasing the serotonin levels of other people but also my own and consequently increasing my enthusiasm.

- Make enthusiasm a daily habit

We are bundles of habits. We are creatures of habits. First, I form a habit, and then the habit forms me. By doing this, I am not only benefiting myself but also other people, since enthusiasm is contagious.

- Avoiding "energy vampires"

These are people who sap my natural energy and strength. I can be sincere and kind when doing this but remain emotionally detached.

- Meditating (even for ten minutes a day)

Doing this regularly will bring about permanent changes in my brain, which will help me to maintain my enthusiasm at peak levels.

- Not only getting enough sleep but also the correct percentages of LIGHT, DEEP, and REM sleep for someone my age and sex
- Moving my body, since this is a powerful mood booster
- Drinking water

I am humiliated to confess that I hate drinking water. I seldom use the word "hate" because it creates negative vibrations throughout my body. and therefore, is detrimental to my health. Having said that as of January 1, 2020 I have been drinking four eight-ounce glasses of water daily. Miracles do happen. Real life is not doing what you like to do but what you need and ought to do.

- Seeing myself with kind eyes

I am aware of my mistakes and attempting to rectify them when possible, but, more importantly, I am focusing on my past and present successes which will spur my enthusiasm, enabling me to do even more.

- Lighting my own fires

    I can light my own fires by doing any task with enthusiasm, with the utmost pride possible, doing it now, and doing it well!

- Emotion management by sending out good vibrations which are simply higher states of vibration

    Being aware of the Laws of Vibration (the feelings that I send out will be returned to me), I daily send out enthusiastic feelings and these are returned to me through matching vibrations.

- Increasing my emotional energy

    Even though I am aware of the value of physical energy, could we be "missing the boat" by putting too much emphasis on physical energy and not enough on emotional energy? The two components of total energy are physical energy and emotional energy. However, physical energy constitutes only a small percentage (much less than half) of our total energy. So, daily I visualize myself living my life with emotional energy. Also, I have been attempting to share my deep dark secrets, since I am beginning to realize the value of opening up in terms of sharing/releasing.

Finally, I am endeavoring to do some new things, since these will increase my emotional energy quickly. Many of the strategies previously mentioned I have been doing enthusiastically, others are quite challenging, and a few I have been pondering, but I wanted to share all of them with you, simply to expose them to you.

Please remember the following quotation by Emerson.

"Enthusiasm is one of the most powerful engines of success. When you do a thing, do it with all your might. Put your whole soul into it. Stamp it with your own personality. Be active, be energetic, be enthusiastic and faithful, and you will accomplish your object. Nothing great was ever achieved without enthusiasm."

FOOD FOR THOUGHT

"Energy begets energy."
Dolly Parton

"Genius is the power of lighting your own fire."
Ralph Waldo Emerson

"The single biggest difference between people who get what they want and people who don't is energy."
Mira Kirshenbaum

"When a man dies, if he can pass enthusiasm along to his children, he has left them an estate of incalculable value."
Thomas A. Edison

"I have found that the myths and unrealistic expectations that society maintains for grievers are some of the worst problems any griever has. If the information you have about grief is faulty or inaccurate, then you risk developing unrealistic expectations about yourself in grief."
Therese Rando

MYTH #9:
TIME HEALS ALL WOUNDS.

REALITY:
TIME, IN ITSELF, DOES NOT HEAL ALL WOUNDS.

When my parents first got married, we lived with my grandparents Cavacini. We took care of my grandmother until she died in her home. When my parents purchased their home, we took my grandfather with us and took care of him until his dying day. When my father was involved in a horrific mining accident but lived for over 30 years, we took care of him until his demise. One word totally describes my father after his accident - TENACIOUS. My mother - willingly and with love - became a private duty nurse until my father expired. When you do anything out of love (as my mother did) rather than responsibility, it makes it so much easier for everyone concerned. To illustrate her total dedication to my father, she sat upright in a chair by my father when he was sleeping. Why? My father had silicosis from working in the mines. He would develop a hacking cough, as he attempted to sleep. He felt that drinking some coffee with whiskey in it would help "break up" the cough. We put a small table with a bell on it near his bed, so my father could ring the bell when he felt he was choking and, therefore, wanted some coffee and whiskey. Since my mother wanted to make sure she would hear the ringing of the bell, she sat upright in a chair by my father's bed. When my mother developed leukemia, Jo, my sister, and I took care of her until she passed in our home on twenty - third street in Windber, Pennsylvania.

Even though my family had encountered grief previously, I was stunned - TOTALLY STUNNED - when JoAnn, my wife and I found Matt, our 20 - year - old son, dead, in his bed, in our home on July 4, 2001. Most recently, my brother-in-law, Ray Wozny and then my sister Jo (taken care of lovingly by Chris Kasisky and her family) both departed from earth. I dedicated my second book to my brother-in-law because, even though he was married nearly 49 years to my sister, we never heard him say one negative comment about her. What ruins any moment is negativity.

What have I been learning through all this?

"We are each of us angels with only one wing, and we can only fly by embracing one another."
Luciano de Crescenzo

The grief recovery process could be the most challenging, demanding, and exhausting work that anyone will ever encounter. We are going to use it to illustrate that time, in and of itself, does not heal all wounds. However, the theme of the quotation about angels covers all segments of our life - not simply the grief recovery process - since we are all in this together, and we can accomplish so much more, when we work cooperatively.

To illustrate, an adroit tribal chief in Africa was concerned about the daily bickering that took place among the members of the tribe. Cliques were forming amid the members which made it much more arduous to accomplish any tasks because of the daily nitpicking. In order to rectify this and bring harmony amidst the tribe, he called a special meeting. In his hands as he was speaking, he had a bundle of sticks that were tied together. Then he asked for a volunteer - the strongest member of the tribe - to come forward. Without any hesitation, a strapping 20-year-old leaped to the front of the tribe. Not only was he six foot seven but also muscular beyond belief. When the chieftain asked if anyone was stronger, the members all nodded in unison that "He was the one!" Then the tribal chief gave him the bundle of sticks that was tied together and asked him to break them. The brawny young man approached this task with the utmost confidence possible, actually being rather arrogant and considered this to be a menial task. However, even though he strained and strained with all his efforts, he was unable to break the bundle. Next the astute tribal chief untied the bundle and asked his frail 93-year-old mother to come forward. He gave her one stick and asked her to break it, which she easily did. The tribe got the message that there is strength in unity. What is true of that tribe is also true of us today since synergy, simply defined, means the whole is greater than the sum of its individual parts. I would have major trouble moving a massive table by myself, but three of us could easily move that gigantic table. That is how powerful synergy really is. If you meticulously watch a flock of Canadian geese, you will notice three traits or characteristics:

Flying in V formation
One "leg" longer than the other
Certain amount of honest confusion

    Scientists have discovered that by flying in a V formation with one of the "legs" longer than the other, a partial vacuum is created. By flying in a V formation, the flock can get to its destination quicker and easier because they are traveling on the thrust of one another. This is also true of people who share not only a sense of community but also a common direction. Why the honest confusion? The head goose is bearing the brunt of the headwind. Before the lead goose gets tired, a member of the formation assumes the head spot. Then the original leader enthusiastically becomes a member of the formation. They take turns doing the arduous tasks. No one bird stays in front all the time.1

Compare this flock to a story about Solo, an individual bird, who decided not to fly south for the winter months. He just didn't feel like flying, not understanding that real life is not always doing what you like to do but doing what you need and ought to do. He stayed behind and really relished a few more sunny days in a farmer's barnyard.

Eventually, as the weather grew colder, Solo realized he had to fly to a warmer temperature if he was going to survive. So, one day he took off to begin his journey all by himself. Remember that the flock can fly quicker and easier because they are traveling on the thrust of one another. Compounding Solo's problems, after several days of travel, the weather began to turn colder. It started to rain, ice began to coat his wings, which made it more and more difficult to continue. Notice, Solo did not have the safety valve of the flock. Desperately, he searched for a place to land and finally spotted a farmer's barnyard. Down he went. He sat for a while; exhausted, unable to move, but happy that he had survived the landing.

    The farmer was cleaning his barn that day and began to shovel some warm manure. A heap of it landed on Solo. Oh, no, he thought to himself, I'm going to suffocate in this stuff. To think, this is the way I am going to die! However, as nature would have it, the warm manure began to thaw him out. He started to feel life returning to his cold little body. Overjoyed, he enthusiastically sang the "Hallelujah Chorus" at the top of his voice.

Would you believe that the farmer's tomcat was resting in the hayloft and heard the bird singing? The puzzled tomcat could not believe that any bird was still around at this time of year. Cautiously he approached the singing bird, found where he was, dug in, and carefully pulled him out. He looked Solo over for a minute, raised him above his head, and said grace. Then he cleaned him off and promptly ate him. [2]

There are many morals to this story:
Not everyone who dumps on you is your enemy.
Not everyone who removes the dump is your friend.
When (not if, because it happens to all of us) someone does dump on you, remain quiet. You can choose to focus on the positives and remain appreciative.

Procrastination is a deadly habit.

We are all in this together, and we need the help and support of other people.

Going back to the flock, what do the birds in the V formation do? They honk from behind to encourage the leader to KOKO (KEEP ON, KEEPING ON). What do you say when you honk? Do you

Complain (These words create negative vibrations!)
Criticize, or (GIGO = GARBAGE IN GARBAGE OUT)
Condemn?

Why should we avoid these incorrect three Cs like the plague? All three are examples of negatives. "What you think about expands." If we concentrate on negatives, we earn additional negatives in our lives. Why not give up complaining or blaming now?

Why not concentrate on the correct three Cs?
Commend, not command (These words create positive vibrations!)
Compliment
Congratulate (GIGO = GOOD IN GOOD OUT)

    We should implement these into our lives because all are examples of positives. If we concentrate on positives, we earn additional positives in our lives. Why? "What you think about expands." Please remember the following quotation by Ben Franklin: "Any fool can complain, criticize, and condemn, and most fools do, but it takes character and self-control to be understanding and forgiving."

    Finally, what happens when an individual goose deviates from the formation? Two geese are immediately sent to lead any goose back on track if they have strayed. If this is not successful, and the goose continues to drift, then all the geese envelop their friend by placing it in the middle of the formation. Notice the power of patient persistence and gentle persuasion. When any bird in the flock gets injured or shot down, at least two members of the flock will stay with the bird until it dies or until the bird is able to return to the flock. Do you have as much sense as a goose?

Also, we can see many other examples of the power of synergy in nature. Imagine that a horrific windstorm took place in a section of New Jersey. All the trees and shrubs were totally uprooted, except for one row of arborvitae. Some scientists got curious as to why only the row of arborvitae was able to withstand the horrendous storm. So, they got permission from the owners of the home where the row of arborvitae was located and dug meticulously around them, only to discover that the roots were intertwined. Thus, as a group, the row was able to withstand the horrible storm, but an individual arborvitae could not have withstood the same storm. Isn't the same true of us; we need the help and support of other people?

These stories distinctly exemplify the significance of effective support groups not only when dealing with grief but in all areas of our lives. Secondly, I have been learning through the grief recovery process (the most challenging, demanding, and exhausting work that there ever is) that time, in and of itself, does not heal all wounds.

About 30 years ago while waiting for my doctor's appointment, a man in the waiting room approached a lady he had not seen in years and stipulated that he hardly recognized her. The dejected lady informed him that her only son had died ten years previously in a horrific motorcycle accident. Since that time, she pointed out that she had lost over 80 pounds, because she has a very poor appetite and sleeps only a few hours each night. She was adamant about never being able to smile or laugh again the rest of her life. Even though it had been ten years since the demise of her son, time did not heal, since she had allowed that event (the death of her son) to dominate her life for the rest of her life rather than (after proper grieving) to continue to evolve upward, onward, and forward, since life is movement.

To further illustrate, devout parents, whose only daughter was killed in a car accident, believed that maintaining a stiff upper lip was the proper reaction to loss. They had been very active in the church and community and continued to be involved rather than taking the time to express their grief openly or even privately with their loved ones and God. These people truly felt that "breaking down" would indicate a lack of faith in God. Not a single tear had been shed! Even though they appeared to be handling their grief well, depression eventually set in, and they committed suicide on their daughter's grave. "Time heals" is not an accurate statement, since we could become sour, disgusted, and frustrated if we do not respond properly to our grief. These religious parents ignored the natural and normal process of grieving. Third, "In the blink of an eye everything can change. So, forgive as often as you can, and love with all your heart. Why? You might never get a chance to do it again."- Unknown Author

This quotation was brought home to me recently when a very close friend of mine died unexpectedly of a heart attack. He was very active, an avid sports fan, and served as a mentor, offering advice and support to many in difficult situations. The week before his death, we had lunch together at a local restaurant. He would give you the shirt off his back, and his legacy to us is the example he set for the rest of us, being a person of integrity who exhibited the proper values, character, grace, compassion, and love that flowed through him to other people. Is this not the greatest contribution we can give not only to our own lives, but also to our families, the world, and to God?

Forgiveness is another key component of the quotation, and, rightly so, because forgiveness is your greatest weapon. You must learn how to operate on yourself and become a judge without a grudge. The final pertinent component of the quotation is the power of love. If I could get down on my knees (At 79 I might not be able to get back up!) and implore you to do just a few things, they would be to live in the now, savor life, really relish life, and to thank God for your life, because no one can take your place. LOVE LIFE, AND IT WILL LOVE YOU RIGHT BACK!

Finally, I have been pondering, because each person's grief is unique, each of us must develop his own unique, effective strategies to cope effectively with it. Remember the Alcoholics Anonymous saying "We are all in this alone… together." When we found Matt, our 20-year-old son dead in his bed in our home on July 4, 2001, I felt the pain of his death very sharply. In the days that followed his death, I felt very sad, but I began to acquire tremendous knowledge about grief and the grief recovery process. Since then, I have been learning, growing, sharing, and reaching out to other people because of this ever-expanding awareness.

"Experience is not what happens to you, it is what you do with what happens to you." Aldous Huxley

When we found Matt dead, I was numb, in total shock (one of God's many protective devices).

After our family made the necessary funeral arrangements, the following day I went to different stores and purchased numerous thank you notes, even though we would be receiving ample sympathy cards from Victoria L. (Bense) Hiteshew, the professional and compassionate funeral director. Why did I do this? I wanted to write personal thank you notes to each person who put her/his life on hold to be with us in our time of grief. As I was writing these notes, I was grateful by the outpouring of love on behalf of my family.

"Although the world is full of suffering, it is full also of the overcoming of it."
Helen Keller

"... Suffering... no matter how multiplied is always individual." *Anne Morrow Lindbergh*

I thanked the people specifically for taking their time - one of their most valuable possessions - to be with us. Also, I thanked them for stopping at our home, for their phone calls, for sending sympathy cards and letters, for dropping off food, and for being involved in the funeral process. Our family was humbled, deeply humbled, by the sincere actions of these fine people, putting their lives on hold to be with us in our time of need.

My last two sentences always were:

"WE SHALL SURVIVE AND BECOME NOT BITTER BUT BETTER PEOPLE, BECAUSE OF OUR SUPPORT SYSTEM, INCLUDING FINE PEOPLE JUST AS YOU."

and

"LIFE IS A SERIES OF MYSTERIES, AND OUR JOB IS NOT TO ATTEMPT TO COMPREHEND THEM, BUT TO BE FLEXIBLE (TO ROLL WITH THEM), AND ABOVE ALL TO KEEP THE FAITH."

    I wrote many letters on consecutive days until I personally thanked each person for being there for us in our time of need. By doing this (writing these sincere letters), I was focusing on the power of gratitude rather than being involved in a continuous self-pity party.

    We know that the grief recovery process takes as long as it takes, but I would like to share with you some specific coping strategies that I have been using. Each of these coping skills applies to life itself.

1. Writing sincere personal thank you notes
2. Continuing to read on the grief recovery process
3. Focusing on deep breathing since this is a simple and effective technique for relaxation that can be practiced almost any time, any place

   The four-seven-eight breathing pattern technique consists of the following:
   - empty air from your lungs
   - breathe through your nose for four seconds
   - hold your breath for seven seconds
   - exhale through your mouth for eight seconds
4. Focus on the moment and being more appreciative of family and friends

5. Staying moderately busy rather than simply "sitting and staring," because our bodies are designed for movement
6. Exercising (stretching, minor weight-training and aerobics) daily if possible and eating healthy foods
7. Saying my prayers in the morning and evening
8. Continuing to have a passion for my work and life itself
9. Finding trusted listeners
10. Understanding that there are certain benefits to suffering such as character development, being more compassionate, becoming a better listener, being less judgmental and having more empathy
11. Understanding I am not in control and turning it over to God (while doing my part)

12. Taking our dog for a walk "EVEN EINSTEIN TOOK TIME TO WALK HIS DOG."

Instinctively, I reverted to my few strong points - reading, writing, exercising, my love for landscaping, and my willingness to share - to help me in my recovery process.

"GRIEF IS A COMPLICATED EMOTIONAL EXPERIENCE."
Earl Hipp

"ALMOST EVERY THOUGHT, FEELING, AND BEHAVIOR IS NORMAL."
Earl Hipp

13. Using my love for landscaping to create a shrub bed in Matt's honor

About one month after Matt's death, Jackie, my daughter, Dwight Kauffman, a true friend, and I created a shrub bed in my backyard dedicated to

Matt's memory. In it we planted and mulched a Sullivan Cypress, a Colorado Spruce, and several Moon Shadows. Each time I walk by this area or see it, or even visualize it, I think of Matt's love for nature. By doing these things Matt's spirit will always be with us.

FOOD FOR THOUGHT

If I Had Known

If I had known what troubles you were bearing,
What griefs were in the silence of your face,
I would have been more gentle and more caring,
And tried to give you gladness for a space.
I would have brought more warmth into the place--
If I had known.

If I had known what thoughts despairing drew you--
Why do we never understand?
I would have lent a little friendship to you,
And slipped my hand within your lonely hand,
And made your stay more pleasant in the land,
If I had known.

Unknown Author[3]

"Sometimes it takes a misguided or false teacher to create a wise student."
Jack Kornfield

MYTH#10:

THERE ARE TWO TYPES OF THINKING.

REALITY:

THERE ARE THREE TYPES OF THINKING.

POSITIVE   REALITY   **NEGATIVE**

THINKING   **THINKING**   **THINKING**

We are striving for *"reality thinking"* where you remain calm, centered, and present. Why calm? Each of us has innate intelligence, an inner wisdom, that can only be unlocked when you are relaxed and calm. Thomas A. Edison stipulated that **"The chief function of the body is to carry the brain around."** Only when your brain is cool can it arrive at the factual conceptual solutions to your problems. One of my favorite quotations is "Don't lose your cool because nothing cooks your goose faster than a boiling temper." Can you now see that ANGER is one letter short of DANGER?

A key component of reality thinking is realizing that - in almost every situation - you will find positives along with negatives, but what do you choose to focus on?

To clarify my point, enjoy the following story:

A powerful king had a humble but learned man as his counselor who had this as his core philosophy: "Don't worry. In almost every situation you will find positives along with negatives. Choose to focus on the positives."

When the king was out hunting one day, the exotic albino deer he had been tracking for numerous seasons got away again. The irate king lost his cool and broke his exorbitant bow in two against a rock. The advisor informed him to look for the positives in the situation. At this point, the king turned his anger toward his counselor, had him locked up in the dungeon and sarcastically challenged him now to defend his philosophy about finding positives, along with negatives, in most situations. The advisor only smiled and stressed the importance of suspending judgment and to wait and see.

The king went hunting again the following day, but this time alone since his sage was in the dungeon. While jumping over a pile of debris, the king was thrown from his horse and broke his leg. When a group of uncongenial men entered the scene, three horrifying thoughts entered the king's mind:

- *Would be robbed*
- *Would be killed or*
- *Kidnapped*

However, when the hostile men noticed his injured leg, the men immediately got on their horses and rode away.

Even though the king was in horrendous pain, he was still able to mount his horse and return to the castle. After his leg had been set, the king called for his advisor to be released from the dungeon and asked him to explain how breaking his leg was beneficial. With a glare on his face, the king, dejectedly, stared at his advocate.

The counselor then explained that those men who approached him were not bandits but did revere the nature gods. These men were hoping to ensnare the king and offer him as a sacrifice to their gods, hoping that their deities would look with favor on them. Therefore, they would reap not only an abundance of crops but also the multiplication of their animals. Since the sacrifices must be unblemished, the advisor pointed out to the king that he was useless to them because of his broken leg.

Now, the king comprehended why the men had pointed at his leg with great excitement, before they galloped away. Reluctantly, the king now "saw the light," but still could not understand why it was best that his guru had been thrown in the dungeon.

The advisor then adroitly pointed out that he always went hunting with the king. If the barbaric men would have seen him, a perfect specimen, they would have taken him, and he would have been sacrificed to their gods. Being locked up saved his life.[1]

Even though we were not designed to be one-dimensional (positive/negative) human beings, it might be prudent at specific times to focus on positivity or negativity simply to regain our balance – "reality thinking." For example, in the 1960s I was at one end of the spectrum, depressed because of my negative thoughts. If I were going to turn my life around and regain my balance, I had to focus on the positives and practice the power of positive expectations. I did this by "shampooing my brain" (washing away the negatives) every morning and then immediately planting "positive seeds," so other negative thoughts could not invade my mind. The "positive seeds" (mental vitamins) were taken from the numerous books that I have read during a 20-year-period. Why read?

"Reading is to the mind as exercising is to the body." – Joseph Addison

Could books be the best source of mind aerobics on this planet? If you want not only to increase your vocabulary but also become a better speller, thinker, writer and speaker, choose to make reading a daily habit, because books can do more for you than truckloads of pills. Imagine reading only five minutes per day which would equal to 28 hours of reading on a yearly basis. By doing this, you can become an educated person without adhering to any formal course of study.

Contrast this (my negativity previously mentioned) with the following incident during the 1990s when I was at the other end of the scale - manic elation or positive thinking. Around 1993, I went into business with three other people with only one goal in mind - to make a massive amount of money. This was one of the few times that I went into any business venture with the sole purpose of earning an exorbitant amount of money and not providing superior customer service at a reasonable price. Unfortunately, as I was blindly going into this business with a more than positive approach, I did not do my homework. Before I became involved in this new business, I should have taken the time to think about what might happen first. Because I was at one end of the scale (manic elation), it would have been smart for me to develop a healthy skepticism (the other end of the gamut) and scrutinize all the possible ramifications of going into this business. Also, I should have used this acronym - TEOWP - to my advantage. Even though it is said, "Experience is the best teacher", that is a fallacy, because experience quite often is too dangerous, costly, and very time-consuming.

Therefore, what is your best teacher - TEOWP (THE EXPERIENCES OF WISE PEOPLE)! You can cut years off your learning curve and save yourself a large amount of hassle and or grief by being receptive to the experiences of other people. Also, I should have checked with a competent lawyer and a certified public accountant. By doing these things, I would have recovered my balance (calm, centered, present and thus reality thinking). Finally, please remember at times you should develop a healthy skepticism and at other times a more than positive approach. Strive for that third type of thinking: present, calm, centered, and right thinking. The trick is to strike a balance between positive and negative thinking.

FOOD FOR THOUGHT

All quotes by Robert Anthony

"If you don't like the games people play, make up your own games."

"Realize that everything that comes into your life is a gift, and that all gifts don't come with a smiling face."

"We dislike our weaknesses so much
that we HATE them
in others."

"Refuse to let an old person into your body."

"Most self - improvement junkies are over - read and under - done."

"Learn to FACE it so that
you can replace it."

"Helping others is the fastest way to get rid of your own troubles."

"Learn to be the rider, not the horse."

"There is no growth without discontent."

"If things don't flow, it means there is more to know."

"Negative thinking is mental malpractice."

"Pay attention. Life sends you a whisper before a shout, a pebble before a brick."

Some people are like cement - all mixed up and permanently set."

There is no reality, only perception."

"Rather than taking risks most people try to softly tip toe through life so that they can arrive at death safely."

"Circle of Creation"
"What we think, we create. What we create, we become. What we become, we express. What we express, we experience.
What we experience, we are. What we are, we think."

DO IT

By:

John-Roger and Peter McWilliams

"There is a myth that in order to reach our goal we must 'think positive' all the time. We don't even have to think positively most of the time."

"To succeed — to fulfill our dream — ALL WE HAVE TO DO IS KEEP FOCUSED ON OUR GOAL AND KEEP MOVING TOWARD IT."

I am both honored and humbled, mainly humbled, to end with not only an exhilarating article by JoAnna Brandi, but also because of its evergreen content, her strategies will never go out of date, regardless of the current news cycle or season. Using these concepts will not only enable you to survive but also to thrive during your adversities. Please enjoy her words that follow.

BONUS
SEVEN STRATEGIES TO OVERCOME FEAR AND PROTECT YOUR FUTURE
JOANNA BRANDI

Should You Believe Everything You Think? No!

I'd like to share strategies I use to overcome the fear and protect my future. They work for anyone.

Be the Witness – Are you thinking or having thoughts? We think 60 to 80,000 thoughts a day; 90% of those the same thoughts as yesterday and 80% of those are likely to be negative.

Thinking is creative. Having repetitive negative thoughts is dangerous because these thoughts activate the centers in the brain responsible for depression and anxiety.

Witness your own thinking and *see what thoughts have you.* Positive thoughts are so much more productive.

Dispute Your Thinking – Once you start paying attention to your thoughts you can start channeling your inner lawyer and dispute those thoughts. Are they true? Are you sure they are true? Who do you become when they are true? Dive deep and find yourself a productive, deliberate, and positive rebuttal to the thoughts that have you.

Adjust Your Explanatory Style – Whether you are a optimist or a pessimist is determined by how you explain the things that happen in your life. Winston Churchill said, ***"The pessimist sees difficulty in every opportunity, the optimist sees opportunity in every difficulty."*** He was right. When faced with a negative occurrence the pessimist sees it as a permanent and pervasive condition and takes it personally.

The optimist when faced with the same negative situation sees it as specific and temporary and doesn't take it too personally. Since how you interpret situations has everything to do with how your body responds to it, now is a good time to make adjustments. The body can't tell the difference between something real and something vividly imagined, so if you want to protect your immune function, adjustments may be necessary.

Reach for A Higher Thought – As you begin to pay attention to your own thinking and observe where it might not be serving you well in this time, add some deliberately positive statements to your mind movie. Thoughts like:

Things always work out for me.

I'm good at what I do.

I enjoy my life.

I am so grateful.

Life is Good.

I am healthy and strong.

I am creative.

> *Your body hears everything you say and responds accordingly.*

Just like you watch your intake of food and add more healthy ones now, so it's important to watch what you are feeding to your mind.

Thoughts cause feelings and feelings cause biochemical reactions in the body. Here's the piece to remember and pull all this together:

Spend 6 minutes in negative emotions and they can shut your immune system down for up to 6 hours. Spend 6 minutes in positive emotions and they will **build your immune function for up to 6 hours.** It's a choice. Over and over, it's a choice.

Ask Better Questions – Every quest begins with a question. We can choose empowering questions or disempowering ones. Empowering questions sound like this:

How can I make this work?

What can make it better?

How can I create more health?

What else is possible here?

How can I create more joy?

How can I set the stage for success?

Stay in alignment with my desires?

Always come out on top?

Disempowering questions sound like:

What's wrong with me?

How come I'm so stupid?

How did I screw up?

Why am I unhappy?

Blah, blah, blah... I'm sure you get my drift here.

Make Space for the Good Stuff – Get yourself a daily gratitude practice. Write down and experience things you are grateful for several times a day. I do that in the morning and in the evening. Keep a gratitude book or a blessings book handy and capture those random moments of gratitude too.

If you are having a challenge with a person or a problem, create a "positive aspects" list where you force yourself to write down 7 things about that person or situation that you can like and be grateful for. This practice really stretches you! For a long time, while struggling in a relationship I had a positive aspects book where I would keep reminding myself of the not-always-apparent goodness of the relationship. It worked!

Learn to deeply savor the goodness in relationship, in food, in nature. The more we stay in the experience of positive emotion, the healthier for our body. Tell others what you appreciate about them. Send an appreciation email to someone new every morning. Send a gratitude letter to someone you've never thanked for something. Spread the goodness!

Get Out of Your Mind and Into Your Body – Move it, shake it, stretch it, shimmy it, get it out of the chair and off the couch. We need to physically discharge the stress from our body or it moves deeply into our cells. Have no doubt about it. We are experiencing collective trauma. When trauma gets stored in the body, it makes for trouble. Don't bottle it up – bust a move, sing a song, <u>dance, dance, dance.</u>

FOOD FOR THOUGHT

"Hate is like acid. It can damage the vessel in which it is stored as well as destroy the object on which it is poured."
Ann Landers

"If you're going through hell, keep going."
Winston Churchill

"Forgive others, not because they deserve forgiveness, but because you deserve peace."
Jonathan Lockwood Huie

"If an egg is broken by an outside force, life ends. If broken by an inside force, life begins. Great things always begin from the inside."
Popsugar

"A ship is safe in harbor, but that's not what ships are for."
William Shedd

"Be who you are and say what you feel because those who mind don't matter and those who matter don't mind."
Dr. Seuss

"With unfailing kindness, your life always presents what you need to learn. Whether you stay home or work in an office, or whatever, the next teacher is going to pop right up."
Charlotte Joko Beck

"In three words, I can sum up everything I have learned about life; it goes on."
Robert Frost

"It's better to be a lion for a day than a sheep all of your life."
Elizabeth Kenney

"I love those who can smile in trouble."
Leonardo da Vinci

"Get busy living or get busy dying."
Stephen King

"To live is the rarest thing in the world. Most just exist, that is all."
Oscar Wilde

"Life is either a daring adventure or nothing at all."
Helen Keller

"Life is from the inside out. When you shift on the inside, life shifts on the outside."
Kamal Ravikant

ENDNOTES

THE POWER

1. Excerpt from *"Fresh Packet of Sower's Seeds"*, 3rd Printing, Brian Cavanaugh T.O.R.,1994, Paulist Press Inc., New York / Mahwah, NJ. Used with permission of Paulist Press, www.paulistpress.com

MY PROMISES TO YOU

1. Dr. John and Pam Carls, The Winners' Journal 2019 (Kalamazoo, MI: Winning Publications, 2019) 90.
2. Ibid., 18.
3. Ibid., 175.
4. Ibid., 172.

FIRST MYTH

1. Charles Jones, "Tremendous," Life Is Tremendous (PO Box 267 Boiling Springs, PA: Tremendous Life Books/Executive books, 1968, 73.
2. ibid., 40.
3. ibid., 40-41.
4. ibid., 40.
5. Reprinted with permission from Jeff Philibin.
6. Earl Hipp, Help For The Hard Times (Center City, Minnesota: Hazelden, 1995) 64-67.
7. ibid., 68-77.

SECOND MYTH

1. Poem on Sharing: Author unknown.
2. Excerpt from, *"Sower's Seeds of Encouragement, Fifth Planting: 100 Stories of Hope, Humor and Healing"*, by Brian Cavanaugh, T.O.R.,1998, published by Paulist Press, Inc. New York /

Mahwah, NJ. Used with permission of Paulist Press, www.paulistpress.com

THIRD MYTH

1. Story about the two shipwrecked men. Author unknown.

2. Eulogy. reprinted with permission from Mary Korzi.

3. "It's all about Jesus." "Used by permission." CD

   Charlie "Tremendous " Jones (Boiling Springs,PA: Tremendous Leadership/Executive Books)

4. Ibid.

FIFTH MYTH

1. Jack M. Zufelt, The DNA of Success, Used by permission (Brentwood: Z Publishing, 2001), 158-159.

2. ibid.

3. The story of the one-armed ten- year - old boy. Author Unknown.

4. Reprinted with the permission of the family of Susan Cook.

5. ibid.

SIXTH MYTH

1. The Story of the Golden Buddha as told by Alan Cohen.

2. Mabel Katz, <u>The Easiest Way </u>(Special Edition) "Used by permission." (Your Business Press, 2009) 37-38-39-40.

SEVENTH MYTH

1. Jones, 36.
2. ibid., 37-38.

EIGHTH MYTH

1. Jones, 22.
2. ibid.
3. Story about the Three Elderly Men. Author unknown.
4. David Seabury and Alfred Uhler, <u>How to Get Things Done </u>Garden City Publishing Co, 1941

NINTH MYTH

1. Story about the flock of geese. Author unknown.
2. Story about Solo the bird. Author unknown.
3. Poem entitled "If I Had Known." Author unknown.

TENTH MYTH

1. Story about the king and his counselor. Author unknown.
2. JoAnna Brandi is a Certified Chief Happiness Officer, a Happiness Coach and Specialist in creating Customer Loyalty and Happiness. She is the author of two books on customer loyalty as well as an illustrated gift book - *"54 Ways to Stay Positive in a Changing, Challenging and Sometimes Negative World."*
She is the creator of the Online Course: *Practice Positive Leadership: Use the Science of Happiness to Engage Your Employees and Keep Your Customers Happy.*

You can find her and her work at
www.ReturnOnHappiness.com
www.postiveenergy.com
www.positivitypractices.com

A very serious effort has been made to locate sources and obtain written permissions to quote when required. Instances of unintentional errors or omissions or inability to find copyright holders sincerely are regretted. Many stories have no sources cited. I presume they are in the public domain, and the author is unknown. However, if a source can be identified, I would be grateful to acknowledge it in the future.

Suggested Reading List

Little Ways to Keep Calm and Carry On- Mark A. Reinecke

Option B- Sheryl Sandberg and Adam Grant

The Power of One- BJ Gallagher and Steve Ruttenberg

1,000 + Little Things Happy Successful People Do Differently- Mark and Angel Chernoff

The User's Guide to The Human Mind- Shawn T. Smith

Keep Calm and Trust God- Jake Provance and Keith Provance

Stress Is a Choice- David Zerfoss

Preach to Yourself- Hayley Morgan

Anxiety Happens- John Forsyth and Georg Eifert

The Bounce Back Book- Karen Salmansohn

I Am Potential- Patrick Henry Hughes

Monkey Mind- Daniel Smith

Life's Missing Instruction Manual- Joe Vitale

Coping with Anxiety- Edmund Bourne and Lorna Garano

Gives Me Hope- Emerson Spartz and Gaby Spartz

All the books written by Mabel Katz

About the Author

Leonard LaPlaca is an award-winning success coach who brings excitement and motivation to life and learning. He has received many awards and recognitions for his innovative approaches to learning. He received an M.Ed. degree in English education from the University of Pittsburgh and a B.S. in Education from Indiana University of Pennsylvania.

He is the author of numerous books and resides with his wife in Pennsylvania where he refuses to slow down. He is at work on his next book.

Made in the USA
Middletown, DE
29 March 2024